Notes From a Concrete Tower: Universities Challenged

By

Tom Spring

British Library Cataloguing in Publication Data.
A catalogue record for this book is available from the British Library

ISBN 978 086071 870 3

A Commissioned Publication Printed by

info@moorleys.co.uk · www.moorleys.co.uk

The views, thoughts, and opinions expressed in this book belong solely to the author, and do not necessarily reflect the views of the publisher or any of its associates.

Contents

Foreword

What follows is an account of a life spent working in the university world. Traditionally the outsider's perception of this world was captured by the phrases "the dreaming spires" (usually Oxford and Cambridge) or later and more generally "the Ivory Towers". But universities in Britain began to change fundamentally from the Sixties onwards. *Brideshead Revisited* gave way to *Lucky Jim* and then *Educating Rita* and the traditional phrases, especially the second one didn't seem to work anymore: ironically that was just about the time that ivory itself became a dirty word and the international trade in it was banned. Good news for elephants and things, not so good for universities since it seemed to signal an actual loss of prestige. The phrase "Ivory Towers" needed to be reimagined since the majority of universities couldn't even aspire to, let alone attain the life of refinement and detached scholarship which the phrase originally signified, at least to the more credulous. By this time there were civic universities, red brick universities, new universities, plate glass universities, campus universities, former polytechnics, you name it. Since I'm chiefly going to write about my experiences in two of these institutions I need to decide the most appropriate noun: what's best to call them collectively? "The Concrete Towers" seems to do the job, capturing the essence of their new functionality but retaining the idea of their remaining a prominent part of the nation's intellectual landscape. I don't mean to imply by the adjective 'concrete' that these institutions were necessarily brutalist or utilitarian in architectural style. Quite a few were but others were architecturally innovative and pleasing and, like the one shown on the front cover, not necessarily made of concrete. No, the word 'concrete' tries to capture the utility and functionality of these institutions. The ancient universities on the other hand, or anyway Oxford and Cambridge, have pretty well resisted the pressures of the modern world and retained much of their distinctive status - just watch an episode of *Inspector Morse* if you doubt this . This is not the world that I write about.

Although my primary intention in writing this book is to tell a story, to write about events and relationships, it behoves me to say at least something about what those inhabitants of the Concrete Towers - like me - saw as their mission in life. I believe they felt it to be about sustaining the cultural heritage that the Ivory Towers represented whilst making it available on a far wider scale and marrying it to a broad range of socially relevant intellectual skills. We all understood that this mission would come under increasing threat both from governments intent on imposing increasingly stringent cost cutting and from meeting the expectations of an expanding client base with a generally more instrumental view of the benefits of education than those who had gone before.

I knew all this, but to be honest didn't really give it much thought. After all, it was never my plan to make the world of the Concrete Towers *my* world. I came from a working-class family at a time when few of us attended university, and fewer still – far fewer – worked in a university. What follows is a set of reflections on my career in that changing world. I make no claim to balance or objectivity, nor do I vouch for historical accuracy especially since I shall be delving back up to half a century. Others would no doubt remember things differently. What's more, I readily admit to having played fast and loose with several of my characters, some of whom only resemble the real people they're based on. I've used them shamefully for my own purposes. What follows represents my own reflections on things, people and events as I saw them, or to be more precise, how I remember having seen them. However it is worth making the point that because of choices made as my career developed, I gained a wider perspective on the world of higher education than many of my colleagues. In short, my head is quite a long way from my bum, so I'm not always speaking through it, which is not a universal characteristic of inhabitants of the Concrete Towers.

So when I say "This is how *I* saw things," I did become a widely experienced observer and participant. On the other hand I was always an untypical university 'don'. I believe, by the way, we're still called 'dons'; no concrete equivalent yet. If you look it up the word has three principal meanings: a distinguished man (especially in the Spanish and Portuguese world), a tutor or fellow at a British University or a senior Mafia leader. Some room for misunderstanding then. However, comparatively few of us are Iberian and even fewer are especially distinguished, and though there are plenty of Heads of Department, Deans of Faculty and especially Vice Chancellors who operate with values similar to those of a Mafia leader, the financial stakes are risible in comparison with the world of organised crime. Deans and so on can sometimes be a little more subtle than Mafia bosses but are invariably less effective. Moreover, it seems you can't have lady dons (only Donnas) though thank goodness there are a lot more women working in the Concrete Towers nowadays. I was often called a 'don', though to be candid that wasn't the only thing I was called.

As an undergraduate I studied Politics and History and then went on to complete two research degrees in Politics, and then I got a job teaching Politics in a Concrete Tower. But insofar as I ever had a plan, that hadn't been it. In the course of my research I frequently met politicians and felt confident that one or more of them would recognise my innate political skills and winning public persona, and arrange to have me offered a safe seat; I didn't mind which party, within reason. Then I would happily bid farewell to my Concrete Tower, collect my lance, saddle up Rocinante and set out to remake the world. However not one of the politicos I met was moved to offer me the prospect of a new career and as one year limped along after another - to the last syllable of recorded time - I had to accept that I wasn't to be a man of destiny after all. And to add insult to injury when in my 40s a graphologist analysed my handwriting she concluded that I lived in the mind, concluding dismissively, perhaps *too much* in the mind. Nothing for it, then, but to stick to the day job. Well, as it happened I came more and more to enjoy teaching Politics and writing about it, so she must have been right.

The story of my career won't set the reader's pulses racing, I promise, but on the other hand, it hasn't been without the odd alarum and excursion and might be of interest to anyone wanting to find out about a don's life, a life that until comparatively recently was portrayed on screen and in print as a bit exotic. Ah, those must have been the days! So: what you have here is a picture of modern university life through the eyes of one who, from beginning to end, saw himself as an interloper. It's organised thematically rather than chronologically, with the first chapter dealing appropriately with examinations, those rocky pathways into and out of the Concrete Towers. After that I'll be exploring the main features of a university don's life, teaching and research, and then I'll have a look at the people who inhabit the Concrete Towers: students, academics and university administrators. Then I want to break away from institutional analysis to devote a chapter to university sport, more precisely to my own sporting activities not because they are especially noteworthy but because sport meant so much to me personally, and after all this is my story. Anyway the universities were the birthplace of the Corinthian spirit that once dominated British sport and indeed attitude to life in general, as Mr. Kipling observed in that famous poem he scribbled on the door at Wimbledon's Centre Court. To complete the picture of my life in the Concrete Towers I shall say something about my research, about the places it took me and the people I met, and how my teaching was influenced as my perspectives changed. Overall the intention is to try to show what life in the Concrete Towers is about, what it meant to me personally and how it shaped me.

Decks now cleared for action, let's begin by getting a hold on those curiously terrifying beasts that stalk the Concrete Towers and indeed most of the world of education, and have recently, though not for the first time, come to dominate public discourse: exams.

1. *Swords of Damocles*

There is a spectre that haunts every middle class and an increasing number of working class homes in Britain; the spectre of public examinations. A bit like the sword that threatened Damocles, exams hang over our heads and bring a sense of dread to our feast. Unlike that frightening piece of well-honed steel however, which after all constituted only a threat, exams are *certain* to crash down on our heads; indeed the precise timing of their descent is known in advance. In the good (bad?) old days of the 11+ we would all sit huddled round the family table on that first fateful morning, wondering who amongst friends and family will survive, maybe even flourish, and who will be cast into what was perceived as the outermost darkness of the local secondary modern. Or later at O or A level, who would be included in the lucky seven per cent whom the sword spared to go on eventually to one of the Concrete Towers – or even one of those posh Ivory jobs. But if you think that the sword that so terrified Damocles had done its work, leaving survivors to savour the exotic fruits of a university education, think again. Three or maybe four years down the line those lucky survivors will be called to account and if they want to leave with a reasonable prospect of earning their own keep, that sword, in the shape of Finals, will comes back to haunt them. And it goes almost without saying a number of other daggers, stilettos and things will have descended on them in the years between getting in and coming out of the Towers.

For many students exams truly were spectral, and haunted their lives for chunks of their adolescence and early adulthood, but for some lucky people exams could prove an exciting challenge. For the most part I loved them, though I have to say that by the time I sat my ninth paper in thirteen days during my Finals at the University of Sheffield I had had enough. Later when I came to reside permanently in a Concrete Tower I worked as an examiner, eventually Chief Examiner in the schools' examination system. I set the papers - hung the sword so to speak - so I took a different perspective. Naturally I had an examiner's role in my own subject area in my Concrete Tower too. In the public sphere examinees were just numbers to us examiners but in the Tower they were well known to us, considered even as friends, which made things difficult, though exam papers became anonymised later.

Blood on the Carpet

How and why did I come to work in public examinations? We needed the money: simples! From the day my wife gave up her teaching job to concentrate on preparing to give birth we found ourselves a bit short of the necessary, and would remain so, for one reason or another, for the next 25 years. I combed the educational press for adverts for school examiners and in 1969 I was invited to mark for an 'O' level Board. It might come as a surprise to anyone who doesn't know it that in England, Wales and Northern Ireland the exam system is managed by rival boards not state institutions. They compete for markets, and competition always leads to greater efficiency - doesn't it? How does an Exam Board establish and expand its market base? The cachet of association with an Ivory, or even Concrete Tower institution helps big time. A strong regional identity is also an asset. Might another way of building a market base be to ensure a good supply of top grades in the results table? If you were the head teacher of a school in a rundown area, you might do a little research to discover which Board offered your students the best deal: which Board failed fewest and gave most 'As'. There was an unofficial league table of Boards and results. Head teachers would realise that though the 'best' universities, especially the Ivory Towers, would know and take account of these disparities when making their offers of places, the great majority of the Concretes wouldn't even *want* to know: for them an 'A' or 'B' grade was an 'A' or 'B' grade, whatever its provenance. To my mind the idea of competition between Boards was obscene but if the system provided me a better chance of getting an examiner's job, I was all for it.

And I did get a job, an assistant examinership at 'O' level, the lowest rung in the hierarchy, and one day in the early summer of 1970, our university term having finished and the marking of our own exams more or less completed, I was summoned down to a meeting in a large

2

hotel in London, one of two dozen or so examiners, many of whom seemed to know each other. We sat in small groups around tables and at the front was the chief examiner, a sharp-featured, stockily constructed Geordie in a dark suit, powder blue shirt and red tie, who sat perched on a corner of his table, He called us to order. We had each been sent a mark scheme through the post, telling us what we should expect in an answer to each question and how we should apportion marks. We had also received our allocation of scripts for marking and our first task was to select about a dozen, along with the marking scheme, to see how effectively the scheme allowed us to assess the qualities of the answers, and to award the appropriate mark, in pencil.

Our business this morning was to go through the mark scheme with the chief and to discuss any issues thrown up by our dry run. The atmosphere was business-like if rather formal and each speaker was referred to by title and surname, and the more experienced markers made useful suggestions for improvement to the mark scheme. By the end of the morning I as a new boy was pretty confident that I knew what to do. Some amendments to the mark scheme were agreed and our business was finished. Now for a good lunch, after which we could toddle off home, with a copy of the amended mark scheme fresh off the press.

Target dates were set for sending a sample of scripts, again marked in pencil, to the chief examiner, so that he could judge how near to the agreed norm we were marking. Some new people might be so out of kilter as to be asked to stop marking there and then and their scripts would be reallocated. For the rest our sample was returned with the instruction to convert our pencilled marks into *bona fide* red biro and continue to mark at our current or a slightly amended level. I was considered to be marking at about the right level. All pretty straight-forward and efficient, I thought. So I was a little dismayed to be informed as the exam period approached the following year that our chief examiner had decided to hang up his biro and we would be under new management for the coming exam.

One warm June day in 1971 I took a crowded early train down to the capital. "Welcome", said our new leader, a youthful looking, bearded sociologist probably in his late forties, dressed in a bold short-sleeved shirt and sand coloured chinos, and wearing open-toed sandals. "I'm *Dr* (emphasised so you didn't miss it) Malcolm Cavendish from Lancaster University. But call me Mal, right?" This, I thought, wasn't just a change in leader; it was regime change: a revolution. The Jacobins had taken over. And indeed "call-me-Mal" made it plain that things *would* be different. First we must all introduce ourselves - and by our first names. Remember this was more than fifty years ago and things were different then. Using first names might have worked for right-on sociologists called Mal with open-toed sandals, but it's a different story if, like one of our markers, you happened to be a fifty-eight year old Deputy Head in a traditional girls' high school who for the last thirty years has been Miss Ponsonby to the whole world but especially to colleagues and students. Miss Ponsonby wasn't a name so much as a persona. Moreover this particular Miss Ponsonby had been christened Priscilla. Identifying herself before us all was like having to take her clothes off. To add insult to injury, as she sat naked before us, 'call-me-Mal' referred to her as Cilla. I felt her pain. I think we all did.

This exercise completed, by which time we'd all forgotten everybody else's name, except Cilla's of course, the Chief explained that we were to begin the day by blind marking duplicated answers to every question on the paper and, through collegiate discussion, arrive at agreed standards that we could all 'own'. Mal concluded with what sounded to me like a calculated threat: we should not expect to be away until 5 pm. Uproar! Many from the north had reserved seats on trains leaving mid-afternoon, several from around London had made other arrangements for the p.m. One large rotund gentleman in a cravat objected, "But look here, Dr....Errrmm... I've committed myself to play in the annual staff-school cricket match this afternoon". "Too bad", says Mal. "Have a look at your contract, Dennis. You're committed for the whole day and paid accordingly". "Well that's as may be...but I've marked for this Board for ten years", says the cravat, standing up and jabbing a plump finger in the general direction of the Chief Examiner, "and we've never gone past lunch – *and* we've always got the job done!" "Well that's not the way things are going to be from now on Dennis", Robespierre replied, "so please sit down and we can get cracking".

Things could only get worse, and they did. We each marked our photocopied answer to the first question, and after about fifteen minutes Mal declared that he proposed to ask some of us to declare what mark we'd given and explain why. This is a daunting task, especially if you are new and more so if you are Sophie, larger than life, or most forms of it, a party girl at heart, bright, but a bit weak on words. And poor Sophie was the first victim. She admitted with a disarmingly vulnerable smile to having given 68%, and explained vaguely how she had arrived at this figure, though on reflection, she added helpfully she could be persuaded to award more...or indeed less. Mal was not disarmed; he was having none of this prevarication. The answer was worth 52%, no more and no less and he proceeded to demolish Sophie's rather limp rationalisation of her mark. The silence that followed simmered with latent disapproval of Mal and sympathy for Sophie, though we soon moved on to question two and the possibility of bridge building.

Mal surveyed his team before pouncing on his next prey, demanding mark and explanation thereof. Norman from Bury, a wiry, thin-faced man with empty grey eyes sat almost rabbit-like in the spotlight. Perhaps chastened by Mal's punitive treatment of the first answer, Norman explained why he had given a mark of 50% to an answer that I was convinced merited more. Mal came down on Norman's rationale like a ton of bricks: the answer was worth 65%. A mark of 50% should simply have been off the radar. Norman had been teaching a long time and had become used to defeats at the hands of pushy younger colleagues, especially in recent years. He sat in resigned silence as his rationale was dismantled. No bridges built then. By now Mal had managed to create an atmosphere of fear amongst the younger and less secure markers and naked hostility amongst the rest. Especially Cilla. And so to question three.

By now Mal recognised that things were not going as he had hoped, and he offered an olive branch: since colleagues seemed unhappy about volunteering their marks, he, Mal, would read out *his* mark and its justification and then ask colleagues for their reaction. About fifteen minutes later he declared to the waiting world a mark of 74% for this third answer. Naturally nobody advanced an alternative view, or indeed any view, so Mal had to prise views out of us. He selected Stuart, another new marker as it happened, from a small private school near Ipswich, who was sitting next to me. I could sense he was dreading the call since he seemed to be trying to hide under the table, but too late: what mark had Stuart given? To be fair, Stuart could have played safe, offered a mark of, say, 70% and basically echoed Mal's analysis. But he didn't. He replied with an apologetic whimper: "Crikey... I only gave it 48%!" Before Stuart had the time even to contemplate suicide others leapt to his defence. Cilla was dismissively on 48% too, and demolished Mal's rationale savagely. "I agree with Stuart. I gave it 50% actually. It was average, so". This judgement was delivered in the kind of Belfast lilt that brooks no argument. Still others joined in with marks around Stuart's, who by now was sitting upright and looking decidedly chipper. Mal tried to defend his original judgement but was simply born down by pent-up hostility. This is not the way things had gone when he'd planned this strategy on the way down from Preston. Silently despairing, he moved on to the next question with the comment that we should all be willing to mark positively and not be afraid to reward originality. Yes, Mal.

The rest of the day turned out to be rather enjoyable. Now nobody was afraid of Mal, and even Dennis-the-Cravat, having missed out on the opportunity of decapitating a few objectionable scholars with his nippy off-cutters gained revenge with a few vindictive body liners aimed at Mal in the rest of a sweaty afternoon. A character in Aldous Huxley's *Eyeless in Gaza* said that in the early stages revolutions are always fun. This one certainly was, though not for Robespierre. We came to understand Mal's revolutionary idea of collegiality: we all expressed our views, had them savaged and then acknowledge that Mal had been right all along. Well that's not exactly the way the revolution unfolded here.

I've no idea whether this chastening initiation into the trials of leadership made Mal a decent Chief Examiner or whether the Board cut its losses, stuck him on a tumbrel and drove him off, Robespierre-like, for the chop. Before the summer was out I received an invitation from an Ivory Tower to mark for them at 'A' Level the following summer, so I left Mal's team. I'd been transferred, not only out but up. Next season I'd be in the Premiership.

The Gold Standard

I had no doubts when I took them and few now, that traditional 'A' Levels provided me with a quality education. They came at the end of two years of study which allowed for a depth that modularisation, when it came, would destroy. In French, for example, we studied not only the language and literature but also the history and culture of France, including French cinema. And my knowledge was assessed in an examination that gave me time to plan my answers before I started writing. Some years later I had the responsibility of chairing the committee that oversaw recruitment and admissions to the University and we had to make a senior appointment of a Schools Liaison Officer. One of our applicants was a young American and to put her at ease I asked her if she'd had time to look around the campus. Yes, although she already knew the institution, she'd come up early to get over to the Students' Union and take in the atmosphere. And you still want the job, asked one of my colleagues? Yes, she much preferred the atmosphere of a British university to the equivalent in the US, the students had more about them. Really? And what did she put this down to? "Oh, 'A' Levels", she replied. "Those guys have encountered culture." Ah well, nothing that a dose of modularisation wouldn't correct a few years down the line. But back to my new job, examining 'A' Levels.

A solicitous elderly gentleman in a starched white jacket took it upon himself to keep our glasses topped up. He looked as if he'd been keeping his own glass topped up before we arrived. Examiners' meetings at Oxford, I discovered, were punctuated by a three course lunch with wine. This was my kind of examiners' meeting. We were a group of half-a-dozen working under the guidance of a Chief Examiner. In his early sixties, he had elegant silver hair that flopped languidly over the top of his pink, comfortable, patrician forehead and rimless glasses from which smiled soft blue eyes. He wielded words like a surgeon wields a scalpel, with dexterity and firmness of purpose. He had about him an easy assurance that one suspected might morph into arrogance when under challenge: there was steel behind those eyes. It did occur to me that he wasn't so much an Oxford don as a film star playing the part of a don, a middle-aged Charles Laughton? Was he any good as a Chief Examiner? Yes, but not *that* good. If his markers were up to scratch he would more or less leave them to it. Of course there were procedures to be followed, deadlines to be met and so on, and here at Oxford we participated each spring in the setting of the paper. On the whole things were measured and civilised.

I made the summer trip down to Oxford many times over the years and honed my marking skills. I would begin marking each answer by glancing first at the concluding paragraph. I'm sure I could have got away with that as a marking technique, just reading that final 'para'. And if an essay began with a sentence including a word like 'ostensibly' or 'incipient ' I would think- just give it a bloody A and get on to the next script. Of course, I never took these shortcuts, but I bet both would usually have worked. The ability to address a question in the broad, understand its significance and *answer* it is one of the most important skills that education can inculcate. Some would argue that having to do this under pressure invalidates the exercise but I don't agree. It's not the only important skill to be acquired. Having to conduct and present a piece of individual research undertaken over a period of time is pretty important too. But planning and writing an examination essay in forty-five minutes or so is a life skill. We have since abandoned it, too much like hard work. A classical scholar once argued that the decline of Rome set in when new recruits refused to train with their regulation shields, their scuta, because they were too heavy. Of course, they'd use them in battles, but why train every day with the bloody things? The rest, as they say, is Roman History.

After a while, about eight years if I remember correctly, our usually genial leader decided to quit and I was approached to take his place. Tricky: I'd only got into marking for the money and whilst being a Chief paid better the workload was much more extensive and would unquestionably be a burden. By now, though, I'd come to see marking almost like a civic responsibility and I knew that I had become pretty good at it. Moreover I enjoyed the company of the colleagues I worked with. So I agreed.

My first task, around February, was to set two papers, British Politics and British Government and Administration, which would then be circulated, along with a paper on American Politics and one on Political Thought set by two of my team, to half a dozen senior markers. Each candidate would take two papers, British Politics being compulsory. A few weeks later we would meet and go over the papers. Were the papers of the usual standard? Did they adequately cover the syllabus? Did they provide scope for better candidates? Did they include words or phrases that might discriminate against disadvantaged students who, for example, might never have come across 'ostensibly' or 'incipient'? And so on. We would agree on any amendments and the outcomes would constitute the papers to be sat the following summer. As time went on, at my instigation, the Board added to its portfolio of papers: International Politics and then European Politics became options, though American Politics remained by far the most popular option followed by Political Thought. Poor old Europe was always to be Cinderella.

After the exam in the summer a few senior markers would be invited to Oxford for two or three days. By this time cost-cutting exercises had been initiated. Gone was the man in the white starched jacket, gone the three-course lunch with wine. We no longer met in the library but in prefabs installed specially in the grounds. Grade boundaries were set anew each year *judgementally* and so the day before our meeting I would be required to look at sets of scripts marked at round about our usual grade boundaries, and to make a set of preliminary judgements on suitable grade boundaries for that year, scripts would be 'pulled' around my provisional boundaries for the team's subsequent consideration

When we met the following day we would first have to agree on the 'A' boundary, and this is where the magic came in. We would first decide what was the lowest *certain* 'A', with no hints of 'B'ness. Supposing we agreed on 72%, then by definition no paper marked lower could be an 'A'. Then we would decide on what constituted the highest certain 'B', with no hints of 'A'ness. (Imagine what fun we had, playing with our 'A'nesses, like a group of fifteen-year olds.) Finally we decided on a mark, let's say 68%. Now we can set this year's 'A' grade boundary, half way between the two 'certainties'. In this case it would be 70%. So scripts already identified as *definitely* not 'A's suddenly became 'A's. This tortuous exercise was repeated at the 'E' (pass/fail) boundary. Again, scripts that been failed magically became 'E's. Then 'Bs' would be decided. ('C' and 'D' boundaries would be calculated arithmetically.) Having worked our boundaries out we would formally present them to senior officers and their statistical adviser for confirmation.

One hot summer we had recommended 70% as the 'A' level boundary for the year. The officers responded that if they were to follow our recommendation, no fewer than 14% of students would be awarded an 'A', whereas the norm was 11.7%. Is there a reason for this discrepancy, they want to know? Have we more 'good' schools on our list this year - i.e. more public schools? Was the paper more accessible - i.e. easier? If you can't explain the discrepancy, the officers went on, we would like you to 'revisit' (weasel word!) your decision. We couldn't explain the discrepancy in these terms and argued instead that some cohorts are just better than others. Not likely, said the statistician, not with these kinds of numbers.

The day is a hot one and the air in the prefab electric. My team insist they will not 'revisit' their carefully considered decision. But this is just what you are employed to do, say the officers, to get the boundary 'right'. I say, as I happen to have said every summer, that it would make better sense to tell me right at the beginning of the process what mark in that year would deliver a statistically acceptable 'A' boundary and then I could look at scripts at and around that mark and with my colleagues confirm or if we feel the need, tweak the boundary. Oh no, say the officers, boundaries must be *judgement*-driven, not *norm*-driven, and that judgement must be made afresh every year – by you. One of my younger colleagues explodes: that's what we've just done, so why not accept our collective judgement? Oh but we will, they reply, if you can explain why it's out of line with previous years. My troops are getting mutinous – they will not 'revisit'.

"Look", I say, "I am employed to set the A boundary. If I am required to set it at 72% then I will recommend this to my colleagues. But we are *not* for 'revisiting'. I refuse to pretend we got it wrong first time." Reluctantly my team agrees to support this line. The officers, however find this unacceptable...but finally accept it. Even they realise that they can't have it both ways. The business wasn't usually this messy but the process invited disputes. To insist that the grade boundaries are established on the independent judgement of the examiners each year is basically bollocks.

But in the words of the song, the times they were a-changing. Competition between Boards was growing and the number of Boards diminishing. Our summer sojourn was no longer taken in languid, leafy Oxford but among the canals of grey, treeless, soulless Aston. Even the sandwiches were appropriately tasteless. Our annual battles had always been about preserving standards, so it was ironic. though this is not the word I'd have chosen, that not long after we moved to Aston, one of the officers pointed out, at the end of our customary labours, that whereas we had awarded about 11.7% 'A' grades this year as usual, some of our chief competitor Boards regularly awarded around 15% 'A's. How would we feel if we too were to award more 'A's, starting right now, and so ignoring the results of the entire laborious exercise we'd just performed and undo, or more accurately, recalculate all the decisions we've just reached? A quick correction to the computer software and Bob's your uncle. After all those battles in the prefab I found this beyond parody. But my team on the whole thought that would be grand: they were, after all, teachers, and whatever meant that more of their pupils would get 'A's, the better. Time for me to go!

The opportunity presented itself the following spring when I was invited to a meeting in Cambridge with the head of the new management structure following yet another amalgamation. I flew down from Scotland, where I was now working, but was delayed by a heavy mist and arrived in Stansted an hour late, with a knock-on effect with my bus connection to Cambridge, and in those days there were no mobile phones. I announced myself with profuse apologies and was advised to get some lunch before meeting the new boss. Five minutes later as I was busy with my soup and roll in the canteen I was summoned by an obsequious minion, whom I knew, to the Boss' room. I replied that I would come as soon as I had finished. "But she wants to see you *now*', said the minion agitatedly. I continued with my soup as she watched in disbelief. Eventually she left. A quarter of an hour later I went up to meet the new Boss. She was crackling with indignation. The epitome of the Thatcherite grey-suited management clone, she was hard eyed, graceless, talking in verbless management speak: in short everything I despised about the new world of management. Since I seemed to find it so difficult to make meetings on time coming from Scotland maybe I should reconsider my position. I replied that I would be delighted to do so. The upcoming session the following month was to be my last.

In my time as Chief Examiner I had seen the traditional 'A' level – the Roman 'scuta' job – replaced by modules, each reflecting at most one year's study not two, and each examined by a shorter paper with shorter individual questions and each offering the possibility of limitless repeats. I had been in charge of setting up one of the first of these new modular 'A' Levels, though as I've said, I'd been personally opposed to the changes. I believe that students have lost something important under the new system. But in championing the old system I have to acknowledge one problem to which I don't have an answer. The influence of a good teacher is of paramount importance. Some schools produced cohorts of students who knew how to plan their essay and answer the question. Not just the good students but the average and below average. The entire cohort would understand what they should do even if some couldn't do it. When you marked scripts from any cohort you were in effect marking the teacher. However that's true of any system, having a good teacher is a game changer. I see no way round that. Nevertheless, I have suggested I would make room for a personal study too, though there are also problems with that.

I had given twenty-four years of service as examiner and then Chief Examiner and found myself wondering how my service would be recognised. A knighthood? Maybe not. Gold watch? I couldn't see it. Some little memento, a farewell dinner and a vote of thanks...or maybe just a vote of thanks? What I got was nada, rien, nichts, zilch, sweet Fanny bloody Adams. Just a brief 'cheerio' just like at the end of every year – not even a 'thank you'. What a beauteous race Thatcher's managers and their minions constitute. That woman in Cambridge wasn't my cup of tea, but I'm sure she has her value. There must be a sewage farm or a prison for hardened criminals somewhere where she could deploy her charm and managerial philosophy to great effect.

The Last Battle

When I became an undergraduate I had been blissfully unaware that degrees were classified. I thought you stayed the course, took the examination at the end and got a degree; or not, as the case might be. True, we had encountered exams at the end of Year One but I had known all about *them*: they were to gain entry to an Honours School I scraped into History and Politics Honours without having done much formal academic work at all. I had been too busy acquiring an education. Too many late nights discussing Really Important Issues. Successfully installed on the Honours course, I thought, I needed only to keep my nose clean for two years and I'd get an Honours degree. It

13

would be impossible today to be as ignorant as I was about these things, but then, I came from a community to whom the word university meant an annual boat-race. I was dumbstruck to discover that degrees were classified and when a friend broke the bad news to me it seemed almost immoral. I'd been having such a good time.

When I became an academic myself, I saw it as my duty, now a new gamekeeper, to ensure that all those idle poachers living a life of Reilly at the expense of the taxpayer should be made to justify their existence in the tutorial room every week as well as in the exam hall at the end of each individual course. At the end of Year Two in most English universities, students had to sit Part One Finals which involved exams in three courses. At the end of Year Three came Part Two Finals. All of these examinations comprised four questions to be answered in three hours – just as it had been in my day and indeed had always been. But it wasn't to last.

For most students, Finals means what it says on the tin, the culmination of your university education. Few in those days, in Arts and Humanities anyway, went on the Masters or Doctoral programmes. Students felt under great pressure to perform and some cracked. Well, you might say, *c'est la vie*: these kinds of situation arise in life and we have to respond. It's incumbent upon universities to make the system fair and equitable, and this is not as easy as it sounds. Degree results are not simply based upon the marks attained in the examination. Departmental Examination Boards will meet to discuss the results and these can be reviewed, especially where students finish on grade boundaries. Let's say Firsts are awarded at 70 and Fiona has a mark of 69. She's borderline. Are there any mitigating circumstances which might persuade the Board to put Fiona's mark up to 70? Each Board will have the assistance of a shadowy figure known as 'the External', a senior academic from another institution, responsible for ensuring some sense of national comparability of standards. The External would have been sent all borderline scripts and been asked for a view on the student. Their word is final, because the record of the Board's decisions needs their signature. They will have been apprised of the various factors weighing in the decision. Fiona's fate will be discussed, often at considerable length, and a decision reached with the External's help. Probably she will get her First.

When I acted as an External I would ask for all failed scripts, all First Class Honours scripts and all marginal and disputed scripts to be sent. I would give a firm recommendation on marginals and disputed scripts but would expect, certainly by the second year of my appointment, to be able confidently to confirm First and Fails with a little less attention, since I would usually be happy to endorse my colleagues' collective judgement. Where I have been surprised by a mark I would explain my misgivings. Appointment as an External would usually be for three or, in Scotland, four years - you'd see a cohort through the programme. In that first year you'd get a feel for the Department's standards. If I felt that a Department was marking severely or softly I would say so, but thereafter wouldn't expect often to be at variance with the internal examiners. Sometimes an individual internal examiner might be out of line with their colleagues and this would have to be pointed out. In my experience Exam Boards were usually happy to be given a steer.

Once a certain English Department sent the last of its scripts off to its External for confirmation, a small package comprising a First and a number of Fails. Several days later back came the scripts with the External's comments. The First came back as a confirmed Fail, an unbelievable and of course unacceptable discrepancy. The Department stood by its judgement, the External by his. Neither was willing to lose face, and there was a lot of face at stake. The Vice Chancellor became involved and the External was 'invited' to resign and a new External was appointed who confirmed the script as a First. What had gone wrong? The original External had worked with the Department for two years and knew its standards. The scripts in question would have arrived when he was up to his eyeballs and he'd probably decided simply to endorse what he thought were the original departmental grades; after all, he knew he could trust their judgement. Unfortunately he hadn't looked too closely at the covering letter and thought he was being asked to confirm a set of Fails. A low-key telephone call from the Head of Department to the External which, without impugning his integrity, suggested the possibility of oversight might have done the trick. But apparently the relationship between the two hadn't been a happy one, and the Head of Department decided to become incensed.

Externals could be a pain. I acted as an External for a professional degree whose breadth of field required the expertise of two Externals. At the Exam Board, as the results were being processed, the other External declared that on principle no examiner should ever award a script below 30%; he never had. Uproar! The intake on this degree course wasn't of the highest academic standard and a fair number of scripts initially marked at below 30% had been elevated by this External, not on perceived merit but as a matter of principle. This was considered to be unacceptable, particularly since that External hadn't raised the issue before. He was pressured into resigning there and then and the Board was obliged to reconvene a few days later, after all his scripts had been remarked.

Externals are nevertheless seldom as big a pain as some Internal Examiners. Exam Boards could become arenas for gladiatorial combat between academics who would oppose each other's proposals on principle. Sometimes favouritism would manifest itself, sometimes Exam Boards for Joint or Combined degrees would excite fierce rivalries between Departments. I recall one Joint Law/Politics student finishing on the cusp of a 2/2 and 2/1. Politics pointed out that the student was a clear 2/1 in all his Politics papers and the Department couldn't countenance awarding anything less. Law countered that for them he was an obvious 2/2 in each paper and they couldn't countenance anything more. The debate raged for a whole afternoon and battle was to resume the next morning. I spent an hour that evening going over the student's Politics record in detail: every essay he had written for Politics over the three-year period had been marked at 2/1. The Lawyers would *have* to give way. I came to the meeting armed with these statistics but in the event the Lawyers conceded the battle without another shot being fired.

When I sat my own Finals I found myself with sizeable problems, but I think I managed to present the examiners with a bit of a challenge too. My problems stemmed from the fact that when as a sixth-former I opted to study for a degree in Modern History and Politics I'd assumed that 'modern' implied twentieth century, or nineteenth and twentieth-century history, like my 'A' level course. Worst case, though unlikely, it might begin with the Tudors. I don't remember reading any information on course content. Moreover because of a motor bike accident I arrived three weeks late and so my course was already seriously underway when I was parachuted into my first lecture which was everyone else's fourth. It was on the nature and practice of *usufruct* and other forms of land tenure. Modern History began in 1066! I was completely gobsmacked and never did get the hang of *usufruct* and the alien world that went with it. I'd just have to read it all up before Finals. But when I came to my Finals revision I'd no notes to revise from, no withered plants to water and bring back to life. I made a strategic decision to concentrate on what I knew and loved – 'real' modern history.

I'd got hooked on the nineteenth century and especially the second half and the rise of socialism. I became captivated by William Morris, and in my revision I followed my heart. Come Finals my deficiencies re. *usufruct* were cruelly exposed but to my joy a question in the Nineteenth Century paper asked us to account for the growth in working-class discontent in the 1880s: *exactly* what I'd hoped for. I had a moment of inspiration. I had been touched by Morris' 'Song to Death', written to commemorate Alfred Linnell who died as a consequence of injuries sustained in the Trafalgar Square Riots of 1887. I thought I could base an answer on the powerful third stanza and so began by reciting it in full and then structuring my answer in four substantive paragraphs plus a conclusion: Each began with a line from the stanza and the concluding paragraph began with the last two lines. I'm confident it was my best bit of writing; I don't think I've ever bettered it.

So how was this a problem for the examiners? Just before leaving the exam hall I looked again at the paper, warmed by a softly glowing sense of triumph. My stomach churned as I now read: "Account for the growth in working-class discontent ...in the 1830s." How *did* they mark that answer? How *could* you mark it? How would I, now, one of the most experienced markers in the country, mark it? Did someone on the Exam Board say that such obvious First Class work simply couldn't be ignored because of an understandable misreading, 3 misread as 8? A mistake anyone could make in the tense atmosphere of an examination hall. And did some younger colleague retort: No, students *can't* be allowed to set their own questions? And after all, subconsciously maybe I *had* set my own question. Anyway, I'll never know, will I? But overall, I did OK. That having been said, I'd have to come clean: medieval land tenure and the specific obligations that went with it have remained *terra incognita* to me.

And how were degree classifications decided anyway in those distant days? A contemporary and good friend was sitting for a General Degree in Arts, which comprised three subjects and was specially designed for future teachers. He was a linguist and one of his three degree subjects was French. Well he passed in each of his papers in each subject, twelve in all I think, but failed the 'Unseen' section in one of the French language papers. And whatever your mark overall on that paper you had to pass that 'Unseen' section to pass the paper, so formally, though he'd exceeded the pass mark he was deemed to have failed the paper. And because he'd technically failed one paper in twelve he failed his *entire degree*. Full-back in the university first fifteen and a player of legendary physical courage, he literally wept when he received his results. He spent the next year earning a pittance as an unqualified teacher, revised like mad, and was obliged the following summer to resit all four French papers. No Exam Board on which I have ever sat would have been so inflexible and if the student body in a modern university had got to hear of such a decision at their institution they would have burned the Admin Block down.

When I was working at the University of Stirling I was asked to sit on a committee that devised an algorithm to calculate all examination results for the whole institution and decide on degree classifications. I knew less about algorithms than I knew about *usufruct* but that was why I was asked to sit on the committee; to represent the peasantry. We were given the task of establishing sets of calculations that could be applied to any departmental degree programme, so that the same set of marks would produce exactly the same result in every programme,. The algorithm would identify those students whose final mark left them on the cusp of a higher degree and these, and only these, would be fully discussed and decided on at the relevant Exam Board which would have the final decision. But even here the regulations strove for consistency: they specified the range of factors that Boards might legitimately consider in their discussions, such as: were there any health issues? How many of the student's papers were in the higher classification? Was the student's performance better towards the end of their course? (This was referred to rather alarmingly as 'exit velocity'.)

This meant the end of those endless tortured sessions, described earlier, where the life history of any number of students might be studied to see if their 'Desmond' (Archbishop Desmond Tutu: 2/2) could reasonably be massaged into a 'Trevor' (Trevor Nunn the famous theatre director: 2/1) and some, though far fewer in those days, would be closely examined to see if their Trevor couldn't be massaged into a Geoff (Geoff Hurst, famous footballer: First.) Parenthetically I find it hard to believe that Scots students would want a Geoff: didn't he score a hat trick in the World Cup Final of '66 for the Auld Enemy? But if they have an alternative, I don't know it. Before introducing our algorithm we mapped it onto the actual degree results of the previous two years and it reflected those results closely, with the exception of one Department which managed to award almost twice as many Geoff Hursts as our algorithm allowed. Our new method worked; at a stroke Exam Boards classified all degrees in less than a day and with no fisticuffs, External Examiners were required to give judgement only on the identified marginal students, and there was an enviable consistency across the institution. It was the most efficient examination system I encountered anywhere and I had been External Examiner at more than a dozen different institutions over the years. Naturally a few years later a new Vice Chancellor and a new management structure abandoned the system as part of a series of reforms.

A post-script on exams. Although I abandoned my 'A' Level marking, I later become involved in some advisory marking for the International Baccalaureate on its extended essay programme: marking the markers, so to speak. I continued to do this in an ever-expanding way for another ten years. A rather different exercise since one's marking team comprised mostly overseas markers and our contacts were exclusively electronic. By the time I decided to quit IB, the whole marking operation was being conducted on-line. Essays arrived on line and were marked on line and one had to annotate essays by selecting pre-cooked phrases. In the attempt to make marking more consistent a template was produced by the Senior Examiner for colleagues to follow. The aim, they said, was to get as near as possible to a model where it was as if Senior Examiners, through their little helpers, had marked every single essay. I oversaw the introduction of this new procedure to Politics for the first year, but it was not a world in which I felt at home. Similar developments overtook university marking about the same time, and here too the system became more electronic and inevitably more regimented, with less room for individual teacher judgement. I'm pleased that I left before these changes were adopted. They represented part of the inevitable regimentation of university education that growing numbers and dwindling resources seemed to demand.

For over thirty years my summers would he interrupted by the ominous thud of packets of examination scripts as they landed on the hall floor. This was never a good experience but just occasionally an exam script or an extended essay would revive my flagging enthusiasm. One short script attempted no answers but instead constituted a virulent attack on the candidate's private school, his Politics teacher, on politics in general and above all upon his father, the driving force behind his school career, whom he appeared to hate with a passion. We were supposed to flag such scripts for the Board's attention but I didn't: the lad seemed to have enough problems. If, on the other hand, his idea had been to publicise his unhappiness I had no intention of assisting. Another script was forwarded to me by one of my examiners, who explained that if he used the agreed marking scheme as directed the paper in question would fail whereas he instinctively thought it constituted a good pass. The essay had no paragraphs, no introduction, no development of arguments, and no conclusion. What it did have was a series of 'propositions': statements which were explored in five or six lines before giving way to another proposition. It reminded me of Wittgenstein's *Tractatus*. All the propositions were relevant and the last in every essay was, in a fashion, summative. The quality of argumentation wasn't brilliant but it was good. I suggested to my colleague that he award a 'B'. He was delighted. In another exceptional and equally unorthodox paper, which I also marked at 'B', each of the answers was written entirely in verse. I wish it had been worth an 'A'.

Two IB Extended Essays, written by seventeen year old lads could have been awarded a First Class mark in an undergraduate degrees programme. One was a brilliant analysis of the geopolitics of the Arctic region by a Norwegian. It was so mature, so comprehensive that I double-checked his sources to make sure he hadn't been plagiarising. The second was written by a Singaporean on the appropriateness of western liberal democracy for developing nations in Asia. It was masterful and concluded by quoting correspondence between Lee Kuan Yiew, the Prime Minister of Singapore at the time, and Indira Gandhi, the then President of India. Recognising the sheer intractability of India's problems, Lee had declared a willingness to offer advice and support. Whilst expressing her gratitude Ghandi had declined the offer; she was attempting to run the largest democracy in the world, he was managing a supermarket. These seventeen year olds must now be in positions of authority in their respective countries. If so there is hope for the world.

For one spell in my career as an examiner and chief examiner I found myself marking scripts from Eton College closely followed by scripts from a college of mining in the north. Not much to choose between the students in terms of quality of argument but in terms of vocabulary and grammatical construction they inhabited different universes.

A final observation: despite all the misgivings about the place of examinations in secondary and tertiary education, when in 2020 public examinations across the United Kingdom were discontinued because of the pandemic, it was heartening to hear the outcry from many students disillusioned at being deprived of the chance to shine.

2. *Teaching in the Concrete Towers*

It was my first meeting of Senate, the body that, in theory anyway, helps the Vice Chancellor to run the university. We new members were greeted by the V C with an apology. He was sorry we had to meet on Wednesday afternoons, but hoped it wouldn't interfere with our plans for the weekend. A joke of its time, it would have no resonance with the staff of a Concrete Tower today. University staff do far more teaching now and are far more involved with administrative matters. Long weekends as a feature of academic life were irregular even then, but at least we knew what they were. When I came into teaching in 1967 my first Honours class comprised eight students, my last, forty years or later, comprised 48. Now classes are even larger. That simple statistic shows how university life has changed. I got to know my eight students, took them out for a drink at least once a term, and had, I like to think, some influence on their intellectual development outside of the formal teaching relationship. Try that with 48 students. A few years ago I met a young academic from Georgia who taught an Honours class of 250: she was visibly on the verge of a breakdown.

At that Senate meeting the VC seemed to be inferring that for some academics teaching was far from their highest priority and that when they weren't formally involved they would be off enriching their lives: weekends in London visiting galleries, seeing plays, that sort of thing. Or just idling around and naturally there was always a bit of that, though nothing like as much as might be supposed.

Old School, Young Turks

When I was a student I was referred to as Mr. Spring and few of my teachers knew anything about me, or indeed wanted to know anything about me, beyond my academic deficiencies. Most of these teachers were scholars and saw it as their responsibility to make their expertise available to those students who were prepared to make use of it. To those who weren't, they owed no obligation. But not many were aware that there were acquirable professional skills that could assist both in delivery of knowledge and understanding, and in assisting its acquisition. Pedagogy wasn't a discipline they were familiar with. One of my History dons would lecture by reading his notes verbatim, with the odd ironical aside, whilst staring fixedly through a side window. And when I say 'fixedly' I mean it; and when I say 'side window' I mean it. All the same I found his subject, the history of the British Empire in the nineteenth century gripping. I discovered later that he was a world authority. But for your average student who wasn't fired by the history of British rule in India or the founding of planned colonies in New Zealand he was probably just a boring old fart. I never got to exchange a single word with the man but I'm assuming that he lived for his research and would have been perfectly willing to make what he had come to know available for anyone who wanted it. I'm guessing the last thing he saw himself as was a teacher. He was a repository of information and understanding.

A young Virginian scholar taught a course in American History when I was a student at Sheffield. He lectured to about twenty of us every Wednesday morning in a small room with a view out over the road. It was at an awkward time and I seldom went. One morning he was talking about slavery and I decided to go, arriving just as he was about to begin. As I entered the room he greeted me in that mellifluous southern drawl: "Well hello Mr Spring. Welcome to my little lecture. I saw you crossing the road just now and thought: isn't that Mr Spring, coming in this direction? He *can't* be coming to *my* lecture. And here you are! I'm honoured. Do make yourself at home." Some lecturers pursued recalcitrants; others didn't, probably thinking that a poor degree would be punishment enough. Teachers offered a resource; it was up to us to make use of it.

Bernard Shaw once memorably declared that those who *can,* do and those who *can't,* teach. This neat little apothegm was augmented, by an irked schoolmaster who saw it as only half the truth at best, with: 'and those who *can't teach* lecture in universities'. Well, in fairness, that did largely reflect my own experience as a student. Yet as universities expanded dramatically in the Sixties the staff profile changed, and discrepancies emerged between the world view of younger and older members of staff, and consequently between their relations with their students. Most of my generation attached more importance to their teaching. I had taken a Postgraduate Diploma in Education, not because I had ambitions to become a teacher, but as a kind of insurance policy in case I found myself looking for a temporary job sometime in the future.

There was an absolute dearth of women in the profession. Come to that, outside of Modern Languages including English there weren't that many female students, certainly not in Politics, apart from the odd Rosa Luxemburg and some early feminists,. And that was pretty much the profile at staff level too. It began to change but only in the late Seventies.

With expansion, younger staff were appointed, staff who like me had experienced the aloofness, even disdain of some academics, and who tried to engage more fully with their students. The situation at your average Concrete Tower in the Seventies was more than a little romanticised by Malcolm Bradbury in his novel, later televised, *The History Man* starring, among others, a youthful Anthony Sher. As Bradbury showed there was a potentially explosive mix with, on the one hand an older generation of established dons committed to their often narrow research interest, some of whom saw teaching as a chore and interaction with students as an occupational hazard, and on the other hand a younger generation much more at ease with the students, having more in common with them – after all they were nearer in age – and more concerned to communicate their expertise to anybody interested. Some of the older dons were notably 'student friendly' - my own career benefited hugely through the help of two - and by the same token, some of the younger ones seemed to aspire to an almost monastic life of dedication to their field of interest, fittingly called their 'discipline'.

Perhaps these differences were manifestations of broader social change. Most of the younger academics, like me, were the products of the sixth forms of state grammar schools where hierarchical proprieties between staff and students were much less formal than in the public schools that had spawned many of the older dons. There were tensions in the expansion that followed the Robbins Report of 1963. What was the purpose of the modern university? Robbins had asked. For hundreds of years universities had catered for a small elite that would go on to run the state and the Church, the professions and even the Empire, which was still a going concern in the early Sixties, or into teaching or academia. The system had expanded in the early years of the twentieth century to accommodate the needs of science and industry through the new civic universities. The Manchesters and Leeds of this world were formally established in those days and though they owed their origins to technical or engineering or medical institutions, when they received their charters they aimed to become 'proper' universities with broader cultural ambitions: civic pride demanded nothing less.

Half a century later, though the ancient universities in England and Scotland maintained a separate ethos, the civic universities were well established and knew what they were about. Or so they thought. Their students would go on to work in the industries of an expanding economy or in the Civil Service managing an expanding state. But this expansion brought a new kind of student, more radically minded, more assertive, and all they wanted to do was to change the world. New disciplines entered the curriculum, or if they existed already, expanded to accommodate these new aspirations: Sociology became the fashionable discipline, Politics emerged, then American Studies (was that a *discipline*?)

We Don't Need No Education

The world outside was changing dramatically and changes in universities were symptomatic of that wider change, and a catalyst for continuing change too. All over the West students wanted to remake the world. Heads were broken; students opposing the Vietnam War were shot in the USA and in France in 1968 students set streets on fire. But Britain didn't have an autocratic de Gaulle to unseat; it had the scheming avuncular Harold Wilson. Moreover Britain hadn't invaded

26

anybody for some time and wasn't involved in a major colonial war, so the scope for revolt was narrower. But that in itself was enough to piss students off, and before the end of my first year of teaching, British universities were following the Continental and US pattern and rebelling. Somehow the evils of Western Capitalism were just as powerfully represented in the structure and aims of British higher education. "We don't need no education" chanted Pink Floyd "Hey, teachers, leave them kids alone!" At Hull, as in most British universities, the rebels wanted first to end American involvement in Vietnam – which manifestly was beyond even them - and second to reduce the number of questions in Finals exam papers from four to three, to space exams out so that nobody got too stressed, and for student representation on the governing bodies of universities to make them more democratic. Difficult? Maybe, but not impossible.

In the battles that followed Hornsey Art College and LSE were in the national headlines for many weeks and for a while even Hull got coverage. There were sit-ins everywhere. At Hull one student, a Politics student of course, symbolically and spontaneously tore up his Finals exam paper with a flourish and a shout of "Down with Indoctrination!" and stormed out of the exam hall. I was there: I can tell my grandchildren. Both Yorkshire and Anglia TV had mysteriously got wind of this spontaneous act of rebellion and were waiting in the car park outside the exam hall so that the rebel could, spontaneously, tear up another exam paper - how did he come by two? - with another cry of "Down with Indoctrination!" just in case it was still being practiced despite his earlier call. He'd be in his seventies by now; wonder what he's up to? Is there a barricade somewhere with handrails? Or is he not long since retired from a successful career in a merchant bank and now living in a delightful Georgian residence along The Stray in Harrogate, wondering how best to finance his grandchildren's private education?

Well, capitalism wasn't brought to its knees and the Americans didn't quit Vietnam for the time being but Hull University did stop asking four questions in Finals Papers and generally made its classification procedures more open and more liberal. And student representation was granted on the main university bodies, such as Senate, and on departmental and departmental committee meetings. As a result boredom and irrelevance were more equally spread. In my experience of the operating of these organs of popular democracy it soon became a perennial problem to find *any* students willing to participate. Forget popularly contested elections; departmental secretaries would have to cajole those they thought cajolable into putting themselves forward. "It'll look good on your CV." On the other hand, academics did generally take more account of student views as a result of '68 and the university system did generally benefit by becoming more liberal.

The ultimate item in the great agenda of eliminating inequalities in education was, of course, the abolition of that most unhelpful of barriers, the one between teachers and students. The aim was to create a level playing field in the quest for greater knowledge and understanding. This required the wholesale jettisoning of 'teaching' in favour of the egalitarian notion of 'enabling'. And why not? After all, we don't need no education.

The ethos of enabling assumes a relationship between the 'enablers' and the 'enabled' that is significantly different than that between teachers and learners. Nobody would have been daft enough to claim that teachers and students were roughly equal whereas enablers and enabled suggests collegiality, the coming together of equals in a joint enterprise. This is a fundamentally different kind of relationship to that of teacher and student. Whereas the latter celebrates the knowledge and understanding of the teacher and requires them to make this accessible to the learner, the former emphasises comradeship on some joint venture into the unknown. I think it's bogus. I've come across innumerable students who had no wish to be enabled and would have far preferred to have been educated. One wrote a short response to a course appraisal question (more on this soon) about the various study skills they had wished to acquire on the unit (note: the title 'unit' not 'course', a tiny example of what Orwell, in *Nineteen Eighty-Four*, called duck speak) in question. "I didn't come here to learn. I came here to be taught." This is going too far, but I know where s/he's coming from. S/he had come to university to acquire knowledge and understanding, to master analytical skills from people who knew more than s/he did. And these were acquired naturally, through transmission in the course of study, not by undertaking some magical mystery tour.

The Transformation of Learning

This venture into mutually assisted learning required academics to produce booklists for each unit so detailed that it was entirely unnecessary to decide for oneself what to read and as prologues to these lists were the unit outlines that all began with a statement of aims and objectives (duck speak) and a mission statement (duck speak). In the real world grown-ups might struggle to differentiate between aims and objectives; indeed we might even wonder why we should bother. However it mattered to the university reformers. Moreover, grown-ups might consider that the aims and indeed objectives for a unit in French politics, for example, would be the same, *pari passu*, as those for German politics. No way! Teachers, (unit co-ordinators in duck speak) had to devise an appropriately gnomic phrase of sophistication and obfuscation to explain what they were about. Different aims and different objectives for different units were essential. I found all this Kafkaesque. As an aside, to my surprise, though not, I suspect, to that of some of my colleagues, I discovered a natural aptitude for bullshit and wonderful phrases that had only the weakest connection to reality just came to me naturally. I like to think of them as comprising an art form closely aligned to surrealism.

In this Alice-in-Wonderland world the *reductio ad absurdum* came some years later when it suddenly dawned on the reformers that enablers could never claim to be achieving their aims or objectives unless they devised a system of student appraisal which could demonstrate that the recipients of enablement had indeed been enabled, or not, as the case might be. My university produced a standard questionnaire for 'unit appraisal' which was about ten pages long and was to be completed electronically in their own time by students on all units. Did the students feel they'd been suitably enabled? Pages of statistics would be generated for the reports, with copies sent to the Head of Department and to the unit co-ordinator, who would then write a report on their report, showing how they intended to take account of any criticisms from the enabled, or more importantly the unenabled. I was given some responsibility, along with the Mad Hatter, for overseeing the results of this time-consuming insanity. I never saw an appraisal from any unit in the entire Arts and Humanities Faculty with a response rate higher than 15%. Never once! Like the appraisal reports, the co-ordinators' responses came to departmental Heads and Deans of Faculty. How many hours were lost to this fatuous exercise, completed every semester, is beyond calculation. And *no conclusion whatever* could safely be drawn from a response rate of 15% max – at best fewer than one in six - beyond the obvious: that neither the enabled nor the unenabled could give a monkey's.

Can you imagine what an effect having to organise all his crap had on the workload of the enablers? But there's more, *much* more. Twenty-odd years after the Great Revolution the University Funding Councils saw fit to examine *all* the paperwork attached to 'teaching appraisal' in *every* university department in the land so that an assessment could be made of 'teaching quality'. This was to be managed by small groups of senior enablers in every discipline who would visit every department and examine all available departmental paperwork over the previous few years. And there were mounds – no, *mountains* - of the stuff. So all unit appraisal reports, all departmental committees' minutes, all aspects of unit appraisal would be gathered together in a document which set out the 'departmental mission' with, of course, details of how it proposed to carry out its mission, what its 'aims' and 'objectives' were.

At the end of this document, departments were asked to make their own judgement as to where their mission was succeeding and where not, and how it was proposed to make good any shortcomings. The head of every department in the country would be obliged to spend half a year preparing a fifty-or-so page document describing this alternative reality. Well of course, no head described their department as failing. But whilst they would signal their achievements on the one hand, they would refer briefly to *challenges* - not failings - on the other hand. And no Head of Department, however dire the situation, would be daft enough to produce a report in which challenges were more numerous than achievements and always these challenges were perceived to be surmountable, Indeed several were already on the point of being surmounted if only the department could be given those extra resources it desperately needed and deserved.

When teaching assessment, as this process became known, was introduced, in the nineties, I was asked to lead the team visit to three Scottish Universities to examine the provision for Politics and International Relations. I measured the thickness of the paperwork that arrived by post from the Scottish Funding Council: It measured just about 80 cms and I and my colleagues in the assessment team – we were four – were required to familiarise ourselves with this for each institution. When we arrived at each we were housed in a room containing mountains of more paperwork: essays from each unit together with the relevant reports from unit appraisal, minutes from the meetings of the several departmental committees including, of course, the teaching quality assurance committee. We met with a few students from each year group to discuss their experiences. Naturally these students were preselected. And we were given four days to master all this material, speak to staff and, crucially, to the students and, *if we wished*, observe some teaching. Remember it was *teaching* we were supposed to be assessing, not mountains of assiduously collected and collated fairy stories written in duck speak.

At the start of each day of our visits I would have a short meeting with the Head of Department. How had the day before gone, they would ask? Did we have all the paperwork we needed? On the first morning at one institution I replied that things had gone well, but could we have sight of the minutes of the Department's Teaching Quality Assurance committee? Of course, he said, though I have to say he looked ruffled.

Next morning, same conversation: still no minutes. Same again on the third morning. Finally on the fourth morning I put it to him that no such minutes existed and that he'd been trying to find the time to create some. Forget it, I said. Just tell me roughly how often it meets, what kinds of thing it discusses, and did he think it was doing a good job? He was mightily relieved and I was happy with his reply, which I reported to my colleagues.

At the end of our visit we would finalise the outline of a report and agree to a judgement under each of nine (if I remember correctly) separate headings, on the basis of which we were to reach an overall assessment of that Department's teaching: was it excellent, highly satisfactory, satisfactory or unsatisfactory? The senior assessor (me for these three) would have to write a report for the Funding Council, with the acquiescence of the other colleagues, giving our judgements under the nine headings and our overall assessment. The senior assessor would then have to speak to his/her report at a meeting of the Funding Council. Before that, however, s/he would have to revisit the institutions assessed and discuss the preliminary reports with the staff, each of whom would have seen a copy of the report. The idea of this meeting was to rectify any factual errors. Significantly those nine individual assessments and the overall assessment were redacted.

It was as if a surveyor sent a report on a property to a would-be purchaser. S/he wouldn't spend so much time pointing out the property's strengths, as the bits that needed attention and crucially would conclude with an evaluation. Imagine turning up at a department with a report that, in effect, concentrated on the damp patches, the broken window sash, the cracked tile on the kitchen floor, without a mention of the property's overall value-for-money, handsome exterior stonework, well-laid out gardens and so on. At the three meetings I went to, every criticism we had made was attacked by the department as factually unsound. These meetings would have been less fractious had our preliminary gradings been made known.

When I arrived a little early to present my first report to the Funding Council in Edinburgh, I overheard the discussion around a report in another subject area. To my astonishment, it sounded tasty, with lots of raised voices: I hadn't expected this. When I finally met the panel I felt decidedly trepidatious. In the event I received only one question. I had referred to a particular problem of access for disabled students. Would I be willing to amend that phrase to students with disability? "In Scotland we like to put the student first, before his/her disability." Who could have a problem with that? There were no substantive criticisms; perhaps the Council members were knackered by then. I've no idea how many forests were sacrificed to the assessment of teaching quality (pre-electronic days) but I do know that preparing for and conducting each visit was enormously time consuming, and of course I had to manage the preparation of all the paperwork for the visitation to my own department.

In truth we didn't assess the actual teaching qualities of any department: we assessed the quality, to all intents and purposes the *quantity*, of the supporting paperwork. It was like Plato's cave, not reality but the laboriously collated representations of reality. Sitting in our chains in the cave, we observed the flickering shadows of the puppets on the wall and tried to work out what they signified. So much easier to turn and face the real thing; we could have handled the sunlight. It would have been better if departments had been given, say, two weeks' notice of a visit – not time enough to prepare paper work - and that much of that visit be given to *observing* teaching as a core of the exercise, *and* *talking* individually to students and staff at our leisure and not just to those preselected for us.

The Funding Councils' intention was to make its assessments available to all schools and to public libraries throughout the land so that the 'stakeholders' (duck speak) and their advisers could make informed decisions as to choice of university. I had an opportunity to 'assess the assessment'. A year or so after, we organised a conference for all Modern Studies (Politics) teachers in Scotland at my own institution. Over 90% attended. How many of these professionals had used the various assessment reports in discussing university choices with their student? Six in just under 100. Later we held one of our regular conferences for students taking 'A' Level Politics (mostly private institutions). About 100 students attended of whom three had looked at the reports.

The Funding Councils must have been aware of the lack of impact of this exercise, as well as the time and financial costs involved, but did they abandon the idea? That's not what reformers do: they pursue their goals with increased vigour. I know of departments which, during a team visit, took steps to 'lose' colleagues whose teaching left something to be desired. One department gave a senior colleague, roundly disliked by his students, a semester's study leave during a visit so that neither he nor his teaching record would be assessed. To be fair, as the recipient of a visit I found some of our assessors' comments incisive and helpful and their report supportive of our efforts as a newly established department. But we could have got those real benefits in a *much* more cost-effective and *much* less stressful way.

Those Who Can't Teach?

I had begun my career with an advantage: as I've said, after graduating I took a one-year diploma course in education. I wasn't impressed with pedagogic theory but I did enjoy my teaching experience, which took me to a primary school, then to a grammar and finally to a secondary modern. The following year, whilst waiting to take up a research scholarship in New Zealand, I taught for a year in a secondary modern in Peterborough. The skills I acquired there, mainly survival skills, turned out not to be useful in a university context. However they gave me confidence in my ability to address large groups of young people several of whom didn't want to be there. They taught me the advantages of communicating clearly and with confidence, buttressed by the crucial advice of a senior colleague: never go into a lecture theatre without checking your flies. I was the only member of a department of twelve who had a teaching diploma and one of three or four who believed that teaching was as important a responsibility as research.

Examination of promotion criteria in universities would tell you why this was so. They were based almost entirely on research records. If you gave a lot of your time to student contact, marked essays assiduously with plenty of comments, you were acting directly against your own long-term self-interest. Promotions to senior lectureship and even more so to professorships have almost universally continued to go to those with a strong research record.

Once I took over temporary supervision of a PhD student from a colleague who was in the USA on a visiting professorship. After a couple of months of weekly meetings the student brought me a draft chapter of his thesis. I gave it back the following week with a couple of pages of suggestions and critical comments. When he came to pick up his chapter he gawped, staring at my comments in disbelief. "Jesus", he said, "when I got my last chapter back from Wadsworth (his supervisor) all I got at the end was a big tick". Wadsworth went on to great things in the academic world - and beyond. The message that came out loud and clear from those universities I got to know was that teaching was basically for losers.

Years later I had an interesting discussion on these matters with a young Russian scholar. I argued that, unlike most of the sciences, so much research in the social sciences and humanities had little value except to further the researcher's career. Scientific research on the other hand might make the world a healthier or safer place (or a sicker or more dangerous one). She argued that research in the humanities was nevertheless crucial. It made us better teachers, and teaching was our primary function. Maybe in an ideal world, I countered, but look where the money supporting our research goes: into large-scale collaborative and preferably multidisciplinary research projects that take the researcher out of teaching. In short, research projects that follow the science–based model but which have little relevance to the humanities and not always much in the social sciences. And these projects certainly won't improve your teaching! I've sat on panels awarding research grants but never saw an applicant advance a case for funding based primarily on the grounds that it would make the researchers better teachers.

This Teaching Game

The traditional model for teaching in the humanities and most of the social sciences has been based on lectures given by the academic running the unit, and seminars or tutorials, in which individual students would read a paper on a specific subject to a smallish group of students and the academic in charge would try to stimulate general discussion. This was the system when I was a student and it had hardly changed when I became a teacher. Normally lectures weren't compulsory though seminars/tutorials were supposed to be. Since it was usual for students to take three courses –units - that would amount to six contact hours per week Theoretically you have to factor in time spent preparing for the seminars, though quite often seminar groups can be dominated by one or two who'd done the reading or who liked to talk- not always the same thing - and those who hadn't, or didn't. If you were one of these you could hide away, unless of course you were the one who had to read the paper that week. Then there's the preparation and writing of essays and that takes a lot of time. True, unlike science-based students, those in the humanities and social sciences don't have to attend regular sessions of lab work, but they are expected to read not just the books specifically related to their courses but also more widely. What makes this more difficult than lab work is that you have to motivate yourself. Or not, of course, in which case it isn't as arduous as lab work. But you *can't* avoid essays. By and large, though, a degree course in the humanities left you room for choice: on how much you wanted to educate yourself.

Let's dig a little deeper. You're not usually forced to go lectures as an undergraduate and if you do you are likely these days to be addressed by someone who will bombard you with bullet-pointed facts on Power Point, facts which you could just as easily glean from a book. You may be lucky enough to get an inspiring lecturer though these days they hardly dare be controversial. The reformers turned their gimlet eyes onto the problem of deadly-dull lectures and produced staff

36

development programmes which gave instruction on how to deliver a lecture. Too often this new development, forced on reluctant academics who were already overburdened with administrative duties, contrived to expand Shaw's analysis to its inevitable conclusion: those who *can* do; those who *can't* teach , and those who *can't teach*, lecture in a university... and those who *can't lecture* in a university run staff development programmes.

Seminar groups once comprised between eight and twelve students of whom, usually, one would have been given the task of presenting a paper for discussion. Every so often the delegated paper- presenter won't turn up because of illness, feigned or real. Usually only two or three others will have done any reading and be willing to lead discussion of the paper. What a deadly way to spend an hour. Now jump forward a decade and the number of undergraduates has more than doubled. What to do?

Many institutions simply doubled the number of seminar groups accordingly, giving the staff an increased workload and employing post-graduates to teach in non-Honours units. Some halved the number of compulsory seminars, making each fortnightly and not weekly. In my own Department we tried to square the circle. Our weekly seminar groups in the first year would comprise sixteen students. They were divided by the tutor into four groups at the beginning of the semester and the weekly topics were divided into four sub-topics. Every week a sub-topic would be assigned to each group. Every week the tutor would introduce the general topic and then the four groups would sit separately for fifteen minutes and discuss their sub-topic, with one student nominated in each group to lead discussion. Then each leader reports their group's 'findings' back to the whole class, relating their sub-topic to the general topic.

By the end of the seminar the topic will have been analysed in detail, with four students playing leading roles and most having been involved in group discussions. By the end of the semester every student will have led their group at least twice. What's more, to ensure that all had prepared for the seminar they would have to provide notes from their reading before discussion began. Seminar performance was graded and counted for 30% of the overall unit evaluation, with 20% for an essay and 50% for the end-of-semester examination. This would only work where strict attendance rules were applied. It wouldn't be worth the effort in Departments that didn't enforce attendance rigorously and there were many who didn't, arguing plausibly that our system was too much like school.

Traditionally students went 'up' to university, even those who lived in Newcastle and went to study in Exeter. And what did they go up to university for? To 'read' a subject. This was probably the legacy of Oxbridge but it seemed to recognise a fundamental truth about traditional university education, especially in the humanities and social sciences, that what you principally did in universities was *read*. The great works of western civilization were there to enrich your mind. I reckon that whilst the state was inviting – and financing - only about seven per cent of the relevant age cohort to come 'up' and 'read' for a degree this more or less worked; it was appropriate for what was, after all, an intellectual elite. The state didn't always invite the right people, it's true, but that's another issue, and there was always an argument for inviting more to benefit from university education. But few universities had adequate resources to accommodate the increased numbers that did indeed come later, and the old model of self-education-with-a-little-help, for that's what it amounted to, was no longer appropriate. What's more the state decided it couldn't afford to finance these new students, so it withdrew grants, though not in Scotland. So an entirely new game emerged: many more students, mostly self-financed and far fewer resources. Some optimists imagined that if students (or their parents) were paying for their degrees they would demand to be better taught but what they really wanted was better degrees and by and large they got them

In the old system the relatively small number of graduates had little difficulty finding appropriate employment. They constituted an elite and were sought after. By and large the intellectual benefits they had accrued from their education were valuable to the state, if sometimes in an indirect way. I found this reassuring as a teacher of Politics. In the early years, though I taught several future MPs and then MEPs and MSPs, comparatively few of my students were looking for a job in politics. What they wanted from their degree was a good understanding of forces that have shaped and governed the modern world. I was confident that that was what we provided, and it made for better citizens. I taught, amongst others, a future archaeologist, a future silversmith, a professional sports commentator and – my proudest boast – a young woman who would become an internationally-known belly dancer. Later, as the subject expanded, so did the percentage wanting a career in politics. I have always regarded this development with anxiety: Has the nation has benefited from the cadre of young Politics graduates who got jobs as research assistants for MPs and went on themselves to become MPs? All the same I believe, and have always believed that a Politics degree provides a broad, modern education, though not as broad as it used to be.

At no point did the state seek to ensure that university teaching programmes matched social needs, even though these needs were more or less quantifiable. Universities sought to offer the courses that applicants wanted. You want a degree in Film and Media Studies, or Tourism, or Psychology, or Sports Science or Law? We've got one! Never mind that our degree structures are designed more to train than to educate, and sometimes to train in skills that are unlikely ever to be useful to the majority of graduates or to the nation at large. Did you know that in 2018, 25% of lap dancers in Britain had a university degree? And not necessarily in lap dancing. Compare this to my one belly-dancer in over twenty years at Hull.

The Duke of Wellington thought his troops were 'ordinary' – actually he was somewhat blunter - adding "it is only wonderful that we should be able to make so much out of them afterwards". Higher Education has seen a transformation in student degree achievement of at least equally remarkable dimensions, judging by degree results: Could it be that when paying over £9,000 per annum (except in Scotland) students and their parents demand to be and are better taught, and respond by working harder? Or might institutions give a much higher proportion of 'good' degrees so that it *looks like* they're teaching better and students are working harder? Despite these reservations, I want to finish on a positive note by declaring loudly how much I've enjoyed teaching in a Concrete Tower. Mostly down to the students, of course.

3. *Research in the Towers*

I stumbled into the Concrete Towers without much idea of what it was all about, apart from the obvious. I didn't appreciate, even when I became one eight years later, that many academics took university posts not primarily because they aspired to teach bright young adults but because they were wedded to some field of research and wanted to be left to continue to explore it with as few interruptions as possible. Monks without the singing or the starched underpants. How on earth - and why - did I enter such a world?

Towards the end of my final undergraduate year, as I've explained, I was persuaded to stay on to undertake a 'research degree'. I hadn't a clue what was entailed but when my would-be supervisor suggested that it would be like being a private investigator I was sold on the idea. But what to investigate? What suggested itself was working on the Labour party but my would-be supervisor persuaded me that the newly invigorated Liberal party offered greater scope for original research. I signed on to do an MA by thesis (as opposed to course work). To those who know nothing about the allure of research, which is the great majority of the human race, I would say it is just as I was told: rather like detective work, piecing bits of information together, conducting interviews with the main suspects, checking the authenticity and value of each nugget of information, and trying to build everything into a coherent narrative. There is a major difference though; your researcher, in the Humanities anyway, always finds the killer and their job is to write a narrative that will convince others. Some years later a new line of enquiry will emerge and a new investigation show that the villain (or hero) couldn't have been the one that you'd fingered. But in academic research nobody gets hanged in error, and other researchers can go on finding new evidence that implicates someone else, or seek to re-establish the culpability of the one accused in the first place, and so on...and on. Few researchers are convinced by the arguments of their competitors and see it as their life's mission to establish their own case, bolstered by yet more research evidence. Finally their work is recognised and they may be awarded a professorship - a Chair - before retiring and then fading into obscurity. Some miss out on the Chair bit and head straight for the obscurity. Research in the Natural or 'Hard' Sciences is an altogether different ballgame, as I shall explain later.

Back from the Margins

I had acquired a reasonable grasp of the history of the Liberal party in my undergraduate days, had read about the "strange death of Liberal England" but hadn't even a vague idea about the post-war fortunes of the party. After the general election of 1955 only six Liberals sat in the House of Commons and only two were English, there because of local agreements in Huddersfield and Bolton, which both boasted two constituencies, East and West. The Conservatives had a free run against Labour in the East seats and the Liberals in the West seats. All four would win. Then in 1956 Jo Grimond, MP for the remotest seat in the UK, Orkney and Shetland (not strictly the Celtic periphery. It's Norse and Lerwick is much further from London - 600 miles – than it is from Oslo - 400 miles) became party leader, and things began to rock. A party left over from a bygone age was miraculously transformed into a modern progressive party that seemed to capture the spirit of the new age more successfully than its bulkier opponents. In 1958 the Liberals won a by-election in Torrington in Devon by 219 votes. It was the party's first peacetime by-election win since the 1920s. The Conservative government of the day, headed by Harold Macmillan, Supermac, was shaken, but with an overall majority of over 60, not stirred. By the 1959 General Election Supermac seemed to have overcome his problems. "You've never had it so good", he told the nation. Gratefully it repaid him with a majority of 100. Yet his authority began to crumble before our eyes and in 1962 the Conservatives suffered a by-election defeat, uncommon in those days, of historic proportions in the decidedly unCeltic constituency of Orpington, in the South London suburbs. What's more the government was defending a majority of some 14,000 and lost the seat to a Liberal majority of 7,000. An earthquake, nothing less. What a time to be studying the Liberal party.

When I had established a working knowledge of the modern party it was time to undertake some interviews. I found this captivating. I interviewed the party leader, most of the parliamentary party, and some key party bureaucrats. I had the great pleasure of interviewing Lady Violet Bonham Carter, Asquith's daughter. I felt I was touching history. A charming woman and a mine of information. We met in her very elegant London flat where I discovered, among many things, that Typhoo isn't the only kind of tea or black the only colour.

Life After Sheffield

It was customary for students on a MA to be transferred to a PhD programme after a successful first year. Without telling me, my supervisor had proposed me for this elevation and Senate had ratified the change. I'd never even heard of a PhD. and had no idea that as far as Senate was concerned, I was now doing one. I had been working on the assumption that at the end of the next year, if all went well, I would be heading out into the world with an MA. As a matter of fact I had a cunning post-MA plan: for my fiancée and me to spend a year school teaching, save as hard as we could, buy a motor bike and just take off round Europe. Some women would have loved the romance of it. Not my fiancée. Her instinctive antipathy to travelling just for the hell of it, or to travel light anywhere, was augmented by the fact that just before coming up to university I had done myself quite a lot of serious mischief on, though mostly off, a motor bike. I had placed myself beyond the pale as far as driving around anywhere on two wheels was concerned, at least if she happened to be on the back.

Talk about serendipity: the very week of our discussion, idly perusing the Department's notice board whilst waiting for a friend, I saw an advert for Commonwealth Scholarships. Apparently if you got one of these you could travel to a Commonwealth country and research for a PhD. So now I knew what a PhD was. I rather fancied New Zealand. Would my betrothed contemplate coming with me to the other side of the world for three years? Well yes, that was a bit more to her taste. Now all I had to do was win a scholarship.

In the course of my research I had come to the conclusion that my supervisor, whilst supportive, didn't rate me as the greatest gift to the study of British politics since Walter Bagehot, so I decided not to ask him for a reference. One of his colleagues took a different line. He had always seemed to enjoy my interventions in seminars, especially the more outrageous ones. He would roll his eyes and say, 'Well *weally*, Mister Spwing!' I would ask him to be my referee. I was called to the Commonwealth Institute for interview. Before setting out for London I had discovered the whereabouts of the Institute and on arriving in the capital on the due date, I carefully studied the Underground map. The Jubilee Line seemed by far my best bet, so I waited...and waited for a train. None came and after nearly an hour I retreated to the ticket office and asked when the next Jubilee train was due. "In about fifteen years mate". If I had looked more closely I would have seen that vital piece of information clearly stated on the map. In the event it would turn out to be sixteen years before the line opened, so it was just as well I didn't wait. I turned up for the interview, a bag of nerves, over 40 minutes late. I was pleasantly surprised they were still prepared to interview me at all but also pretty sure they'd reject me. But no: I was offered a Commonwealth Scholarship.

At the end of that academic year I decided to leave and find a teaching job, to earn some money, expecting to finish my MA part-time. Finding a job turned out to be no easy task, to say the least, but eventually I did, and in the nick of time, the week before the new school year started. The school, a Secondary Modern, was in Peterborough, a place I'd never been to in my life, and teaching there was a revelation. I was asked by one class if I was Swedish; apparently I 'talked funny'. I didn't get much chance to explore the area since in the evenings I'd work away in my digs on the MA.

Regularly, about once a month, my fiancée and I would drive up to Sheffield and stay with friends for a weekend. On the Friday early evenings I would see my supervisor. At one such meeting I informed him that the following summer I would be going on a Commonwealth Scholarship to 'do' a PhD in New Zealand. He literally jumped: "And what would you want with two PhDs?" "But I'm registered for an MA here", I replied. "No, you were transferred to a PhD last month by

Senate." "But why didn't you tell me... or better still, ask me?" I replied. "Because that's what always happens if we think you're doing well. And you have done well. You'll get your doctorate." "Well we're all geared up to go to New Zealand now, so please can you arrange to transfer me back again to an MA?" He wasn't pleased but he should have known enough about me to have appreciated that I wasn't *au fait* with the 'normal procedures'. Another thing that my supervisor kept from me: he personally paid my registration fee for the MA degree, and no doubt would have done so for a PhD.

When I'd applied for the scholarship I had to identify a proposed area of study and I thought that since New Zealand had a two-party adversarial system just like the British, with a small third party just like the British, I could transfer my finely-honed research skills into this new setting with minimum fuss. After all, the two parties were Labour and Conservative (National): piece of cake. The head of the Political Science Department at Victoria University in Wellington with whom I had been in touch before my interview thought so too. During the course of the next year, however, he had written suggesting that I consider an alternative field of research, in case there should be 'problems' (unspecified) with my chosen area. Plan B could be, if I wanted, a biographical study of a former leading Labour politician. I liked the sound of that, and readily agreed.

We set sail in August 1964 from Tilbury Docks two days after our wedding. Life at sea allowed plenty of time to revise the completed draft of my MA, so I was confident that five weeks later, on arrival at Wellington, I would be ready for an assault on the NZ party system.

The Land of the Long White Cloud

Two days after arriving in Wellington to grey skies and a chilling wind, and having been met on the quay by an anonymous looking, monosyllabic Head of Department, I was invited to a Political Science departmental meeting. To my surprise the entire teaching staff was present at this meeting. Moreover the Head of Department wasn't in the chair: he was stuck away in a corner and hardly acknowledged me as I came in. The

45

chairman introduced me to all eighteen present, identifying the man who would be my supervisor. Then he asked about my proposed field of study. I looked across to the Head of Department for a lead: he said nothing. I launched confidently into plan A only for it to be promptly and comprehensively savaged. Social Credit, New Zealand's third party was a Mickey Mouse outfit, I was told, that didn't merit serious academic examination. I caught the Head's eye, he looked away. "So", said the chairman, after an embarrassing delay, "any other ideas?" This time I opened with a defensive gambit. "Well, the Head of Department suggested a political biography of Walter Nash." No way, they said to a man - no women present. You couldn't possibly write a political biography for a PhD in Politics, or, significantly, Political *Science*, which specifically required a theoretical framework. "So what *is* this chap going to do?" asked the Chairman.

Had we been in Manchester say or Leeds, 'this chap' would have replied: "Well, I'll tell you what I'm going to do: go home – and by the way, thanks for nothing!" But we'd just travelled nearly thirteen thousand miles from the other side of the world and going home was not an option. A longer, even more embarrassing silence, then, almost discursively, my putative supervisor, asked: "So what have you been doing with yourself over the last year then, Tom?" I told them about the MA thesis, explaining rather plaintively my interest in third parties, and then mentioned that I had taught for a year in a secondary school. His eyes lit up. "That's it, everybody: The Politics of Education! There's a PhD field if ever I met one." To a man (still no women) they agreed. The Head of Department uttered not a word. This is not how things are supposed to happen.

That first year in New Zealand turned out to be among the worst of my life. We were a long, long way from home, family and friends. I had nowhere to work and was struggling to get a hold on 'my' research topic; after all I knew literally nothing about it. I had one advantage however, without which it might have broken me. There had been a bulky Royal Commission report published on the administration of education only a year previously and it provided a full description of all the major bodies involved, so all I had to do was master a full Royal Commission report to know what I was dealing with. I said earlier that a PhD in Political Science is supposed to make some contribution to analytical theory, to construct a model, in this case of decision making. Now models in the natural and physical sciences are generally replicable, reliable and testable, whereas your Political 'Science' theories can't be replicated, aren't always reliable and can almost never be tested; everything in politics is contingent. The philosopher Karl Popper had been pretty clear on this, and he had spent time in New Zealand, so he should have known. Here I was alone in a small room in a faraway country, trying to construct an abstract theory about the workings of a system of which I was utterly ignorant whilst believing that at the best of times such theories were largely without value. At one stage I thought I was beginning to lose my marbles and went to see the local doctor. He told me I was working too hard: take two weeks off and get out more, he prescribed. Could I read, I asked? Yes, but *not* about work. I went to the nearby Botanical Gardens every day for two weeks and, under generally sunny skies, amidst exotic flora, I immersed myself in Jane Austen. I read all the major works; felt much better and never looked back: Jane Austen, much better than pills. She should be free on the National Health.

Slowly things improved. First, relief was provided by a trip to Sydney. My Master's supervisor back at Sheffield had arranged an oral examination for my MA with a Professor at the University of Sydney, conveniently only 1,386 miles away. I had five pleasant days in Sydney and came home with an MA (Econ). Back in windy Wellington my supervisor introduced me to people in the NZ Council for Education Research and they found me temporary office space. I was able to talk to knowledgeable people about what I was doing on a daily basis. By the end of that first year I was increasingly confident that I knew what I had to do and this transformed my world.

In our second year in New Zealand I acquired a room to myself in the University library building. This was an amazing facility that any postgraduate student would give their eye teeth for. By this time I was becoming better known amongst the people involved in the running of education and I was given wide access to people and papers. Towards the end of this second year I began to think about completion and about going home. Though we had become content with our lot we wanted to return. My handsome scholarship had been for three years and I presumed that I had to have everything done and dusted by its expiry. That would see us getting back to Britain by late autumn of 1967, my third year. From an employment perspective that was not so good. If I were to look for a job in higher or further education I needed to be home before the end of the current academic year, to secure a post for the forthcoming year. What I didn't know – how *was* I to know since nobody saw fit to tell me? - was that it was *assumed* that I would be applying for a year's extension to the scholarship: indeed it was budgeted for. The fourth year would be used to write up one's thesis. A fourth year in NZ would have been fine by us: finishing by April 1968 wouldn't have been a problem. But I went for completion in April '67 and put myself under huge pressure.

The external examiner for my viva was a fellow Yorkshireman and things seemed to have gone well when he casually remarked that, of course, the conceptual or theoretical frame, which had given me so many problems, would need to be dropped. He actually used the word 'junked'. Nonplussed, I reminded him about the required theoretical dimension. "Yeah, but that's for your PhD" he said. "But isn't that what this is all about?" I asked plaintively, my whole world on the point of implosion. "Well no. I'm talking about a potential book, not your bloody PhD. I've no problems with *that*." So we left Aotearoa in late March 1967, just over thirty months after arriving. I returned six months' worth of scholarship money. I would pay for this Herculean effort later. Cleaning the Augean Stables and doing all that other stuff would have been a piece of cake by comparison. (Not too sure about the lion though.) For the next two years at least I frequently thought I was losing my sanity. At concerts I found myself wanting to jump up and yell in the quiet bits. This was not a good place to be. Nobody I knew had finished a PhD so quickly, though I understand that Robert Mugabe's wife managed hers in five months. Children, don't even try this at home.

Back in Blighty

I spoke earlier about academics being absorbed by an area of research to which they would happily dedicate their careers. For most that area naturally grew out from and built on their PhD research. Not me. New Zealand education wasn't a suitable field for an academic in a British Politics Department to be cultivating; neither could you teach a Politics Honours option for undergraduates on it. As for my earlier interest in parties, especially the Liberals, most Politics Departments in British universities had experts in British parties coming out of their ears. This made me a bit of a risky appointment: I was well qualified, with two research degrees and two published articles in learned journals, but what would I contribute in the future? Fortunately the department at the University of Hull took a punt on me. But what field of expertise was I going to command? And what would I teach?

As it happens, I was lucky in my colleagues. One of the activities I had indulged in during my research was reading widely. For example I had read all of George Orwell's books and most of his essays, and I happened to get into an argument with one of my new colleagues on interpreting some aspects of Orwell's work. He was generally far better read than I, but not regarding Mr. Orwell and my arguments impressed him. He subsequently arranged for me to give a paper to the departmental staff/student society, the Machiavelli Society, on *The Politics of George Orwell.* I have to say immodestly that it went well and I was subsequently invited back over the next couple of years to present papers on H.G. Wells and Bernard Shaw. My colleague subsequently suggested that I prepare an Honours option on Politics and Literature. That was over thirty years ago and though I have also researched, taught and written on British political parties, Politics and Literature has been my prime area of research interest and I have been happy to give a chunk of my life to it; my wife claims that Mr Orwell has been the third party in our marriage.

This is what research means to most academics and the opportunity to pursue a research interest is what still draws young hopefuls to apply for academic posts even when they have far less time to do their research than we did and when the administrative pressures on their lives are substantially greater than they were on ours. Recently I was chatting to a young woman in her final undergraduate year and happened to ask whether she'd made any plans for her future. She told me that if her degree was good enough she would return to the university and take a taught Master's degree, she knew already what she would write her dissertation on. If successful she then planned to proceed to a PhD and had identified an area that she would like to specialise in and had held discussions with a putative supervisor. Her objective was to teach and research at a university in the general area of Human Rights. In my experience this degree of forward planning is pretty typical nowadays. It represents the polar opposite of my own trajectory in just about every aspect.

The Research Industry

The purpose of research degrees in the Humanities, then, is primarily to provide a career path for future academics. I earlier likened research to detective work and an important aspect of the comparison is the importance to both of analytical skills and individual initiative. Good detectives and accomplished academics would have said that these were skills that couldn't be taught. This is no longer believed to be the case regarding academic research or indeed detective work so far as I can make out. Nobody taught us how to 'do' research. We had a supervisor, an expert in our field, who would offer advice and give feedback on any work you put in front of them. If you didn't put work in front of them at regular intervals, good supervisors would chase you up. But not all; some were unwilling to apply pressure either because they were busy with their own work or as the result of some romantic notion about the impossibility of jump-starting creativity. Or both.

In those days when I became an academic a research student would have no formal commitments outside of their research and since most were on grants sufficient for them to continue to live at the kind of bohemian level they had enjoyed as an undergraduate, there was always the option to drift along waiting for the muse to move them.

50

Able students who got their act together would traditionally finish their research and write it up in four years or so; others, having enjoyed state support for these four years, might never finish. This was intensely irritating to their supervisors and indeed to the university but never a major problem for funding bodies because in the Humanities only a small number of scholarships were awarded in the first place. All the same it was wasteful and inefficient.

My first experience of supervising a research student wasn't a happy one. The student in question approached me in his final year as an undergraduate and told me he would be applying for a university research scholarship for the next academic year and would like to work in the area of Liberal party politics; would I write him a reference and supervise him if he were successful? I was young and inexperienced at the time and lacked the confidence to tell him that I didn't think he could manage a research degree: after all, I was only six years older than he was. Besides, I was confident that he wouldn't achieve a good enough degree to win a scholarship, so I reluctantly agreed. Well, he got an Upper Second, but it was marginal and in normal circumstances he wouldn't even have been considered for a scholarship, especially since my reference hadn't been enthusiastic. To quote Billy Bunter's Indian chum, the normalcy of circumstances at the time couldn't have been terrific: to my amazement he got the scholarship and I was appointed his supervisor.

Over the next year he subsequently submitted several pieces of work, which, in principle, might have formed parts of thesis chapters, but none was well enough written or sufficiently analytical. His sentences lacked structural coherence. It wasn't possible to recommend the extension of his scholarship into a second year. Maybe he would develop intellectually later; but I thought at the time that the University did him no favours in awarding him the scholarship. I let him down because I hadn't the balls to be straight with him from the outset: I hadn't wanted to hurt him. In effect I stood by while he hurt himself. In mitigation I had made my reservations clear in the reference, and in a normal year he wouldn't have been made an award.

Another early experience as a supervisor was equally unproductive. A bright young woman wanted to write a thesis on the politics of William Morris. Her application for a scholarship was unsuccessful but she managed to fund herself for a year. I was happy to supervise her. In the course of that year of research she read prodigiously but wrote not a single word. Periodically I would call her in and we would discuss her lack of progress and I would set and then reset a timetable for submission of draft chapters. I tried to stay supportive and encouraging but as time wore on I became progressively less sympathetic, progressively more critical. We later agreed to call it a day. Sometime after, a friend of hers told me that during the year she had indeed read widely but simply couldn't find the confidence to write anything. Apparently she loved it when I told her off and the more critical I was, the more she loved it.

After these disasters things could only get better and when in due course more responsibility came my way I was able to make changes to the way the Department managed postgraduates and their research. For example, to build their self-confidence and instil the feeling of being part of community, as well as earning a little money, all research students were required to do some monitored first-year tutorial teaching. In addition to a personal supervisor each would have regular meetings with a small departmental research panel to discuss progress. I was confident that this would strengthen the relationship between supervisor and student and deadlines would be more rigorously applied. Moreover the Department ensured that every PhD student had office space. None of our post-grads suffered as I had in my first year at Wellington.

Regime Change

As universities expanded in the late Sixties and Seventies and became more expensive to run, the government, which after all footed the bill, tried to ensure better value for its money, in research as well as teaching. Universities had traditionally been funded via the University Grants Committee, established just after the First World War. The science subjects have a distinctive research model that usually involved a senior academic running a lab with a number of research students working to solve specific problems as part of a team. They would research what the supervisor required them to research. If the project were deemed to have been successful the senior researcher would be allocated bigger bucks for the next project and each of his/her research team would be awarded a PhD. Many such projects thrived on international and sometimes interdisciplinary collaboration. At Hull, for example, the Chemistry Department won the Queen's Award for Industry for its pioneering work on liquid crystals, scattering PhDs like rose petals as it went. Governments could confidently fund this model and derive a tangible, measurable gain.

In the Arts and the 'softer' Social Sciences, usually collectively called 'the Humanities', this model didn't much apply. Here research was often undertaken by an individual working on archival and interview material. S/he might find it advantageous to collaborate with colleagues overseas, or with colleagues in other disciplines but not necessarily so. More important than the *modus operandi* though is the appropriateness of measurable social benefits. How much does society as a whole benefit from a new interpretation of Charles Dickens' alleged misogyny, or of the origins of Prussian militarism? And if the government were to fund such projects, which should it choose and on what grounds? And who would – *could* - declare this kind of research successful?

Governments frantically trying to secure value for money began to apply the science model to the Humanities, first to the Social Sciences collectively, where in some circumstances they were inappropriate. Some worthwhile scholarly activities required nothing more than time and good libraries or archives. With the improving inter-library loan service a researcher might be able to do much of their research at their own establishment and at little cost. What was certainly not in the interests of such scholars was that they be obliged to follow a pattern of research enquiry that aped the Natural Science model. Yet this is what happened.

In 1965 following the election the year before of Harold Wilson's Labour government, and responding to Wilson's call for a white hot technological revolution in all aspects of the British economy, a Social Science Research Council (SSRC) was set up to oversee the funding of research in that area. To be funded by the Council research in the Social Sciences needed to be focused on some concrete social good. (For example, a colleague and I were awarded funding for a project on parliament and health policy.) But if your research was chiefly archive or library-based the work of the Council wouldn't affect your life much. You would get time off from your own university and if you needed funding to attend a conference or to access a distant archive, it was possible to get it from your institution or from private sources.

The Transformation of Research in the Humanities

In 1979 Margaret Thatcher became Prime Minister and she and her mentor and Minister of Education.Sir Keith Joseph decided to cut funding to this apparently economically unproductive area of research and abolish the SSRC .Thatcher, it's worth pointing out, was probably the only British PM to have a scientific background, having worked as a research chemist for ICI, and Keith Joseph's full title was Minister for Education *and Science*. They were dissuaded from outright abolition and settled instead for a revamp: SSRC made way for ESRC. Social scientists everywhere expressed their anxiety that the new ESRC, shaped on its science equivalents, would impose models of scientific research methods on all, regardless of their appropriateness. Rubbish, said the ESRC representatives, who were sent round campuses to dispel such anxieties. D'you take us for philistines?

In a short time a new breed of younger social scientists emerged, adept at constructing research projects involving their mates in Europe and the US, which would require massive surveys and quantitative, comparative analyses of parties, bureaucracies, institutions, NGOs or whatever. They seemed to be writing papers and books not so much on the subject of their research as on their research *techniques*, especially those involving data analysis. I attended a series of seminars in France on European political parties in one of which a senior German social scientist produced a raft of statistical evidence to show that governments who weren't able to control their parliamentary timetable were more legislatively productive than those who were. The ensuing debate was entirely about the statistical method and analysis the project had employed. Nobody at any point questioned his general conclusion, though any sane observer could see it was nonsense. This whole exercise, the project and the dissemination of its findings, was funded from the public purse. On another occasion I went to a seminar in Glasgow given by a friend on voting behaviour and electoral outcomes. I arrived early to find him writing an equation on the whiteboard. I watched in awe as it spread inexorably along the wall like a fungal growth. I asked him what the equation was about. "Well", he explained, "it shows that all things being equal, the incumbent party will usually win an upcoming election". "But Aristotle", I said (not his real name) "things are *never* equal, are they?" "No, 'course not. But you can't factor that into the equation." And he was right: reality's a bummer. Let's just stick to talking about techniques.

These research projects, especially if they embody the right buzz words such as interdisciplinary, collaborative, international, ground-breaking, policy-related, almost invariably cost squillions. Of course they don't all fit this pattern, but many do and the relevant periodicals where accounts of these great ventures are written up parade a morass of vocabulary and grammar which would leave the uninitiated splashing around desperately looking for something solid to hold on to, so as to haul themselves up onto the terra firma of reality. More often than not though they drown. W.H. Auden once questioned whether any amount of 'scientifically' garnered data such as I'm referring to here could ever compete for insight with the "single intuitive glance" of the writer. If there is clear evidence that large-scale research programmes sponsored by the ESRC have been successful in advancing our knowledge and understanding of politics, I've missed it. But in monopolising funding streams they have been largely successful in marginalising traditional individual research in the social sciences.

In more recent years this 'science model', having laid low some of the social sciences, has turned its attention to that other branch of the

Humanities, the Arts, where the main criteria for funding research are now couched in the same kind of science-orientated vocabulary specifying similar outcomes whose worth can chiefly be measured in terms of some definable social good. Fortunately those allocating funds in this areas - and I've been one - know that a scholar can profitably spend three years studying some canonical text from the mediaeval world that might - *might* - transform our understanding of, say, the sale of indulgences. Such a study would fall short on most of the criteria used when the Arts and Humanities Research Council decides whether to fund it, and to stand any hope of success the case would have to be advanced with all the right buzz words. If the applicant had an established international reputation, it could still get funding. But in future?

Researchers in the 'hard' Sciences have normally been able to show the efficacy of their research model. It has been to the detriment of some Social Scientists and most researchers in the Arts and Humanities that they too are now constrained by the same model. It hasn't been shown that society or the economy has benefited in any way from remodelling research in the Humanities; it is certain that no public money has been saved. Quite the reverse.

Researching What and for Whom?

Which leads me finally to consider a general problem: how we go about assessing the value of research in the Concrete Tower so that it can be properly funded? And there's a prior question here: *why* is research in the Concrete Tower officially assessed? For the 'hard' sciences the second question is easy to answer: research in the sciences costs mega bucks and is potentially beneficial to society. Scientific research in the universities *matters* and its successes and failures can reshape the world. Look no further than Oxford's involvement with Astra Zeneca in proving an effective vaccine against Covid 19. Since government provides much of the funding for this kind of research it has a duty to ensure value for money. That's why scientific research needs to be assessed, so that funding goes to those who can demonstrably use it well. But what about the Humanities?

The contribution of research in the Humanities to the social good is generally far more obscure, more likely to be observable only in the longer term and always difficult to quantify. I don't include the likes of Psychology, Social Psychology or Criminology whose work can often fall into the category of 'hard' science. Comparatively speaking Humanities research costs peanuts. Hence the significance of the prior question: why should governments involve themselves in research activity whose 'successes' are almost impossible to quantify, especially in the short term, and whose impact on the national economy, also in the short term is insignificant?

Traditionally university staff were paid on the assumption that they spent 60% of their time on teaching, preparing, delivering, marking, student welfare, and 40% on research. Just after I started back in the days of the second Wilson administration, a large survey was conducted by government on how dons spent their time. A random sample, which happened to include me, was asked to keep a diary allocating their time on a half-hourly basis through the week. Cynics believed that the government wanted to establish that in the course of the academic year those in the Humanities spent a disproportionate amount of time on unproductive research, augmented every seventh year, in most institutions, by a term's study leave, known as a sabbatical. Sabbaticals weren't automatically granted and were often attached to administrative duties. (On my first sabbatical I was asked by senior university officers to write a script for a university film to be used in student recruitment. It took almost the entire term. Sabbatical leave often turned out not to be what it said on the tin.) In the event the government's survey established something quite different: we in the Humanities were not squandering time on unproductive research. The disproportionate and growing usurper of dons' time was administration. Research had become a pleasurable hobby fitted in where possible but mainly in the vacations. The survey's findings sank without trace.

Science research councils would 'buy out' key researchers by making funds available to their universities to appoint new colleagues on a temporary basis to do their teaching. When the ESRC, and then the

AHRC (Arts and Humanities Research Council), were up and running they did the same, but that funding tended to be geared to large collaborative projects that followed the science model. The whole exercise began as a way of controlling expenditure on research in the Humanities and finished by substantially increasing it. In the process they severely constrained the traditional scholarly research undertaken by individuals which had cost only slightly north of sod all. Now we know more about the 'Why?' what about the 'How'?

.

Well, the research assessment process was similar to that assessing teaching quality which we've just considered, though it predated that exercise. The Research Assessment Exercise (RAE) was first conducted in 1989. Each discipline, such as Politics, had a panel of experts drawn from senior members of the discipline who were asked to consider and assess the research output of every Politics department in the land and to grade them from 1 (lowest) to 5 (highest). Each department would submit a long and detailed report listing the publications of their staff over the previous five years. They were also asked to provide a narrative of the general research infrastructure of their university and, in a supporting narrative outline developments that might have affected their productivity over the period: age profile, such as long-term staff illnesses or pregnancy leaves, departure of staff and so on. With all these relevant data you might have thought the exercise pretty straightforward. Think again. Significantly, you can't easily compare large departments with small ones. A single pregnancy leave or long-term illness might distort the research profile of a small department. Moreover the effect of different age profiles can't easily be compared. Those, especially smaller departments, with a significant number of younger members are at a disadvantage. For obvious reasons nationally and especially internationally rated research is usually a badge worn by established academics. Such structural differences make genuine comparisons almost impossible. And they uniformly disadvantage small departments.

But there are additional anomalies that tend to disadvantage smaller departments in assessment. If a colleague in a small department makes a significant contribution to their research field they may be 'poached' by a larger department. Well, that's life; eh? Winners tend to move on, just like in soccer. However when Jarrod Bowen moved from Hull City, where he had been Player of the Year, to West Ham United in January 2020 for £25 million, the Football League didn't deduct any of the 18 goals he'd already scored for City that season and donate them to the Hammers. But that's precisely what happened in the RAE. If the 'rising star' of a small department moved to a larger British institution, in the next RAE half of their 'goals' (research publication) go with them. The 'donor' department is allowed to record only half of their publications though *all* of these publications - 'goals' - had been scored whilst the star was with them, despite the possibility that the team strategy of the donor department, especially if it were small, might well have been geared to maximise the potential of their star at the expense of others. Moreover, if the rising star is poached by an overseas institution, the original department gets to register *none* of their publications in its report. And as if that weren't absurd enough - but it is - the smaller department, unlike the Hull Cities of this world, receives no transfer fee at all. OK, they can usually replace their stars but seldom timously and *always* by lesser stars. After selling its star forward by the way, Hull City, at the time handily placed in the top half of the table were relegated at the end of the season, even though all of Bowen's goals were included in their statistics. At least Hull City received substantial financial compensation to spend on replacements, whereas in the university world the 'donor' department received exactly diddly squat. Enough said?

The consequence of the RAE, then, was to reinforce the prejudice in favour of larger research projects associated with larger departments. This had been the intention: to concentrate research in so-called "centres of excellence". Yet to the extent that the exercise 'worked', it must have harmed the *raison d'être* of university education, which explicitly links teaching to research, and it completely disregards the likelihood that the atmosphere created by a vibrant, research-active small department will be more supportive of its student body than that of a larger more amorphous department whose 'stars' are often elsewhere. On a visit to the University of East Anglia once, in the late

'80s, I saw a piece of graffiti on a toilet door in the English Department. It asked; "What's the difference between God and Professor Bradbury?" It helpfully provided the answer: "God is everywhere, and Professor Bradbury is everywhere but here." Small can be good and worth nurturing. Those God-fearing Government Ministers and officials concerned with this exercise knew their Bible. Matthew 25:29 reads: "For to everyone that hath shall be given, and he shall have abundance: but for him who hath not shall be taken away even that which he hath."

But even on these dubious terms, can research assessment work? The quality of a research outcome in the Humanities can only be judged several years, maybe decades after publication. Inevitably the RAE tends to measure quantity rather than quality. Heads of Humanities Departments and Deans of Humanities Faculties become reluctant to encourage colleagues to involve themselves in projects that would be likely to require years of individual research the true value of which *couldn't* be apparent before the next RAE. This produces an obligation to publish for the sake of publication. A normally productive scholar caused incredulity and despair amongst senior university officers assessing his department's research performance when he responded to the challenge that he hadn't published *anything* in the previous academic year with: "Well, I didn't think I had anything to say." What world was he living in? Learned articles aren't about contributing to scholarship so much as providing a measure of activity to be counted.

I've considered research in the Concrete Towers in this chapter, and the attempts to measure its success. It's a crucial indicator of how university education has been changed, in my view for the worse and for the wrong reasons. I want to change focus now from activities to personnel and to consider first not what academics do, but whom they do it to: the punters.

4. *The Tower Dwellers: Students*

Students differ in every measurable respect. Their reasons for choosing to become students, the pathways they trod and the difficulties they encountered on the way all differ. Probably most important of all: what they take away with them when they leave, what they have become, also differs. The more you know about them the more you can help switch them on. Never easy, even when numbers were manageable, but in their final year, when your relationship to individuals is a key to their development, it becomes virtually impossible when you have an Honours class of forty to fifty.

Getting to know your students is important; getting to know them in the biblical sense, however, isn't generally a good idea. I would be lying if I said that such thoughts hadn't crossed my mind, but early moral conditioning - Biggles and Baden-Powell - and a lack of confidence in my own personal charms kept me chaste. Only once, when a former nurse from Liverpool whose essay I had recently failed, came to see me, exposing enough of her breasts to recommend a remark, did the possibility present itself unambiguously. I moved round her to open my office door wide continuing the conversation, which she chose to curtail shortly afterwards. Sometimes trying to adapt to the needs of individual students isn't a sound idea.

Too Clever by Half

There are other occasions when one can take the attempt to get on the same wave-length of individuals too far. Once I taught a lanky second-year undergraduate with a Forces background. He spoke in that clipped, matter-of-fact manner that you associate with the officer class. He aspired to a modest level of academic competence and displayed a distinct lack of enthusiasm for serious engagement, not uncommon in the student body. This resolute disengagement would manifest itself in irregular attendance at tutorials and only spasmodic attempts to engage in class discussion. When he missed two consecutive tutorials without explanation I thought he needed a strong word. I checked with the departmental office to see if we'd any notification of illness – we hadn't – or whether he had been missing other people's classes – he wasn't. So I wrote him a letter trying to capture his own uncompromising way of speaking. I told him that the only acceptable excuse for missing two consecutive tutorials was death, imagining, as I wrote this, his responding with a soldierly guffaw as he read it.

By return I received a letter from his father telling me that the lad was fighting for his life - meningitis. The parents had been poleaxed by my letter which, wrote the father, would have been callous and unprofessional at any time but utterly repugnant in the present circumstances. Had I taken the trouble to check, he continued, I would have discovered that the lad was unwell at home and had missed all his recent classes. He was minded to complain officially to the Vice-Chancellor. I can't put into words the explosive effect that this letter had on me. I had tried to write in a style tailor-made to bring the right response from his son: I would have, and indeed often had written differently to others in a similar position. What's more I knew that the letter was incorrect in both fact and interpretation: I *had* made the necessary checks and he was wrong about his son's attendance. So I wasn't concerned about the possibility of any official complaint; what utterly overwhelmed me was the effect that my letter had had on those grieving parents.

I wrote back immediately, of course, offering an unconditional apology and only at the end did I mention that his criticism of lax procedures had been unfair. I received no reply but there was no formal complaint. The lad recovered and eventually completed his degree. In normal circumstances I'm sure my letter would have had the desired effect but we were where we were, as they say, and over thirty years later I remain full of remorse. There's a lot can be said for good old formality.

Sebastian and the Arrows

As I've already explained, as a student I'd no idea that degrees were classified. You either got a BA after three years or you didn't. Things changed and by the time I was teaching, all students knew how the system worked and many of them thought they knew how to play it.

Some years ago a survey was done on the death-rates of grandfathers of university students which showed a remarkable proclivity on the part of grandfathers – almost never grandmothers – to peg out around examination time, requiring their student grandchild's presence at their death bed, or funeral. Unfortunately, but quite coincidentally, they consequently would have to miss exams or deadlines. Sometimes though students scaled far greater heights of imagination. Sebastian, a student from Birmingham - "Sutton Coldfield actually" -came to see me just before Part One Finals, at the end of his second year, to give an account of the acute pressures he'd had to contend with over the course of the academic year, pressures which he believed might affect his performance in the up-coming exams. It transpired that a long-term relationship had been terminated dramatically by his partner just before Christmas. For several weeks he'd been devastated, but worse was to follow: his former partner, she who had dumped him for another, informed him by phone shortly after his return that she was pregnant. Sebastian had to buckle down to his studies with this news hanging over him. He thought long and hard and decided he would stand by her despite her earlier treachery. He made a short trip back to Birmingham - Sutton Coldfield actually - and they met. There was a tearful reconciliation, and when he left to return to university their relationship seemed even stronger. So strong that she felt able to break the news a month or so later that the child wasn't his. He asked me to imagine his feelings as he rushed back home... again. He still loved the girl and convinced himself that he had the moral fibre to stand by her. After all, a child was a child and so he arranged a meeting, where tears were shed and promises made. Nobody else knew of the turmoil he was going through but their relationship, if possible had become stronger than ever.

Shortly after Easter vacation, and just two weeks before the first of his examinations, she phoned to tell hum curtly that she'd decided to have an abortion and thought it best to end their relationship. "She knew I was a Catholic; she knew what I felt about abortions. And she knew what I felt about her." Could there have been any more angst left in his angst-tank? There needed to be, because a few weeks later he discovered that she had begun to see her other gentleman friend again. So perhaps I could understand, he concluded, why he hadn't given as much attention to his studies that year as he would have liked. This dramatic saga was told me in the strictest confidence; I wasn't to speak of it at the Exam Board under any circumstances. Should he happen to finish on the cusp of a classification, say between 2/2 and 2/1, he knew that it couldn't formally be taken into consideration. But maybe, he helpfully suggested, I could refer obliquely to 'extenuating personal circumstances' that indicated his performance had been materially affected, and that elevation to the higher classification might be considered. It would have been a problem, asking a Board to take circumstances into account of which they knew nothing. On the other hand I was quite senior by now and my voice, I think, and I think he thought, would have carried some weight. In the event however his marks overall averaged at 55%, so he was nowhere near being considered marginal and I decided there was no point in my saying anything.

If you have tears, prepare to shed them now. We are at the Exam Board meeting the following year: Part Two Finals. Sebastian is sitting on 59% and so would automatically be considered for elevation to 2/1, which was a good degree in those days. In the ensuing discussion on Sebastian one of my senior colleagues, a decent if ingenuous individual, admitted to being in a quandary. He told us that he was privy to some crucial information about Sebastian which, though he had given his word not to divulge details, would, convince *anyone* that this apparently marginal mark represented a triumph against a series of awful adversities. He hoped that we could back his professional judgement in this matter and elevate Sebastian to the higher class. Understanding and supportive nods around the table.

After a brief silence I felt I had to say something. Whilst we might all appreciate that our discussions couldn't go into detail concerning this sensitive case, I said, and whilst none doubted our colleague's judgement on its merits, might I nevertheless hazard just few general suppositions? For example, might we suppose that this list of awful adversities revolved around the fracturing of a long-term relationship...

and maybe a pregnancy? My colleague's eyes popped and his jaw dropped, and that's not hyperbole. How did I know, he asked, when he'd been sworn to secrecy? I offered a few other salient details: it turned out to be almost an exact repeat of the previous year's list of tragedies. Poor Sebastian; like his canonised namesake, martyred not once but twice. So many arrows, so many cudgels. Our task wasn't to assess Sebastian's moral status but his academic performance, so his tutors gave reports on his work during the year. In fact there was no evidence to justify elevation to a higher degree, and as you might imagine, no desire to do so without any such evidence. He left us clasping a Desmond, though no doubt he went on to a successful career in the world of high finance... or politics... or something of that nature. I've since checked another awful possibility, but thanks be, he never became a Cardinal of the Church.

Choosing Winners

It was the Department's custom, in my first year in post, to interview prospective candidates, and even we new teachers were involved, though always in tandem, never alone. We interviewed one young gentleman with an exotic name and some individualistic views on the nature of society. My fellow interviewer, a political philosopher, had just completed the purchase of a pleasant semi-detached house out in the East Riding. He was rather pleased with himself, and couldn't help but bring the interview round to house buying. In these interviews we always got round eventually to discussing some non-academic topic. House purchase, though, wasn't a subject that many students would have had views on but our man had strong views on everything and let rip, attacking those pretentious 'little people' who contented themselves with living in a semi. He could understand those who bought a terraced property: they knew their place and just got on with life. High achievers on the other hand, would settle for nothing less than a large detached property, even if they couldn't afford it. But the second-raters who bought semis – weren't they just signalling a lack of ambition and a willingness to accept second best? He despised them.

Far from leaping to the defence of these middle-class second-raters, whose ranks he had just joined (and I aspired to join before long) my colleague drew the student out. There was no real intellectual substance to his assertions, however, just as there hadn't been to anything else he'd pontificated on in the course of the interview. I was unimpressed. When we discussed him at the end of the interview, however, my colleague was convinced that we had to have this man with such original and deeply held views. So refreshing. I recognised masochism when I saw it and anyway, I think part of him felt that the student was probably right. It would have been unreasonable given our disagreement to reject his application and so we agreed to recommend a standard offer and sure enough he duly appeared in September. He went on to make no contribution to departmental life and left us three years later with a standard degree, leaving no trace. I had been right and my colleague had been wrong.

Except about ten years later when I was watching the regional news I saw an interview with one of the local MPs from a near-by Tory rural constituency. It was our man! I'd been wrong after all. At the following general election however he managed to lose the seat. No – I'd been right. Then a few years later he won the much coveted Tory nomination in a by-election in a safe Tory seat in the South of England. It looked like I had been wrong after all. But in the subsequent by-election, at the height of the Poll-Tax conflict, he contrived to lose one of the safest Tory seats in the country. There. I knew it! However he subsequently became a successful barrister specialising in family law and a figure of some note. I'd have to admit that on balance he proved me wrong after all.

Best of Mates

The University of Hull operated a scheme of buying and customising nearby terraced houses to provide university accommodation. In those days a member of academic staff would be appointed to act as a kind of warden to around half a dozen such properties. They didn't 'live in' but were required to visit regularly and to make themselves available should there be any personal or disciplinary matters to be resolved. Each house would contain around half-a-dozen students, with one older student being nominated as 'senior', operating as a kind of liaison with the relevant member of staff. I took on this wardening responsibility, which was paid, though not much, for several years. In one of 'my' houses were two Politics students, close friends, both of whom I taught. Angela, from East Anglia, was tall, fair haired, and of a matronly disposition. Samantha, a Geordie, by contrast had sharply chiselled features, black hair and deep green Irish eyes. Angela was totally committed to her studies. Always in the library, she would trawl through most things on the reading list and make copious notes, and produced reliable but uninspiring essays. Samantha on the other hand floated serenely above the surface of the work ethic, yet always got to the heart of any issue with genuine forensic skill.

Late one November afternoon Samantha knocked on my office door to tell me, very matter of factly, that her friend Angela was pregnant, would I talk to her? Next day later Angela herself duly arrived, with her mate for moral support. I wasn't sure what she expected of me; maybe she didn't know herself. She'd been to a party and one thing had led to another, as things often do. No question of an abortion, no question of involving the father. There was nothing I could do but then, as they say, they also serve who only sit and listen. I did advise her strongly to let per parents, especially her mother, know before going home at the end of term. This, my single piece of advice, she flatly ignored. However I was able to reassure her that I would take care of the academic side of things.

Angela didn't appear at the start of the Spring Term. Samantha came to tell me that the baby had been delivered safe and sound but that Angela hadn't even seen it. Her parents had been completely supportive from the moment she appeared at the door. The decision to give the baby up had been her own. She returned a couple of weeks later and was soon back in the rhythm of university life, working as hard as ever, though to no better effect. Maybe she'd lost a bit of her bounce.

Finals results were pinned to large boards in the main hall in those days, so you had to jostle with the madding crowd to discover your fate and to share it with everyone else. Angela got the expected 2/2, her mate a good 2/1. Ironically Samantha, who'd plans to work in jewellery design, really didn't need a good degree. Angela, on the other hand, *so* wanted to get a research job with an MP and would have given her eye teeth for a 2/1. I don't know what happened to Samantha but I suspect Angela would have found a placement with an MP somehow; after all, she had a lot to offer, not least perseverance. I felt privileged to be taken into the confidence of these two young women, though I'd felt about as useful as a chocolate fireguard....

More to it than Teaching

Towards the end of one summer term, my wife was due to take a school party up to Bempton Cliffs, which would mean her leaving the house at 7am, so I was to be in charge of rousing the children (we had two boys at the time, aged seven and five), preparing breakfast and taking them off to school. So we were early to bed the night before. At around 2 am the phone went. It was the senior student from one of my houses, an all-female house: could I come round as soon as possible? One of the girls, a Brazilian post-grad, had attacked her room-mate with a pair of scissors. No serious injuries, no panic, but the girl still had the scissors. I biked round like the wind.

By the time I arrived what hung in the air was shock rather than fear. The young woman in question was still brandishing her scissors. I asked her to give me the scissors, but she just pointed them at me, swaying. She looked so fragile and I knew that if I blew hard she'd fall over. I told her quietly that I was going to take the scissors from her because her friends were concerned. She made no attempt to stop me. She sat down, crumpled, on the bed and the senior girl sat down quietly next to her put her arm around her. She turned to me with a look blank despair.

I got the full story. There had been an argument with her room-mate in the small hours, and she'd half-heartedly stabbed the girl in the arm with those scissors, which she'd picked up from the kitchen table. The stab mark – Exhibit A Your Honour – was certainly visible but didn't deserve anything more than the antiseptic wipe it had already been

68

awarded. The senior was apologetic about involving me but she thought she ought. I asked why she hadn't phoned the Medical Centre for the on-call doctor. But she had, and the doctor had declined to come out at that hour for what he deemed to be a non-emergency.

This annoyed me and confident that the crisis was over I phoned the Centre and spoke to a chatty Irish nurse who confirmed what had happened in respect of the doctor. I asked her to phone the man again and tell him that the responsible academic, who *had* come out, had suggested that he come out immediately to deal with a medically related emergency. He did so, arriving towards 4.30. As soon as he arrived I left, stopping to make the required report at the Medical Centre, but not before telling the doctor, in private, that his failure to make himself available was inexcusable. We didn't part on the best of terms.

Later that morning the mental hospital - it had been shown on my 1967 Ordnance Survey Map as the County Lunatic Asylum - acquired a new inmate, a young Brazilian woman who stayed for several months before flying home with her father. I later discovered that on the day of the incident she had been informed by her department that her course grades weren't good enough for her to continue to the dissertation stage of her Master's course. Her father, whom I later met, told me that she had boasted to the family of how well she'd been doing, but that in her more recent calls had seemed depressed and reluctant to discuss her work.

In those days overseas students, by no means as numerous as in later years, were mainly post-graduates. If you came as an undergraduate you had to have a recognised certificate of proficiency in English before receiving the offer of a place. Bizarrely this was not formally required of post-grads at the time, with the potential for the kind of consequence I've just recounted. Post-graduate students from overseas on taught Masters' programmes meant big bucks and some universities were unscrupulous in making offers. Perhaps some - how can I put it? - might have occasionally put too much faith in their teaching colleagues' ability to make silk purses from sows' ears? In my department we seemed almost permanently to have a group of South Korean military personnel on our International Relations programmes. I had nothing to do with these students when I was Head of Department other than greet them officially. One year however one of that cohort came to my office towards the end of the summer term to tell me he was leaving. His performance on the coursework over the year hadn't been of sufficient standard for him to continue to the dissertation over the summer. That would mean leaving with a Certificate and not a Master's Degree. His Commanding Officer in South Korea had ordered him home with immediate effect. I commiserated and asked what he proposed to do on his return. That, he said, was already decided. He would be confined to barracks until he had saved enough from his army pay to meet the costs of his 'failed' year at Hull. Then he would be dismissed. What a miserable outcome. If he felt sorry for himself it didn't show.

There were a handful of individual South Korean undergraduates in the Social Science Faculty at Hull too, and how alien everything must have seemed to them. They sometimes unwittingly fell foul of British social conventions. One student in his forties and well-heeled was 'invited 'to leave his hall of residence because he used to look into women's rooms with powerful binoculars. He explained that this was important preparatory work in establishing which women he wanted to have sex with. When it was pointed out that this was not the custom in the UK he was affronted. We didn't seem to understand: he would offer them a *very* satisfactory financial arrangement for their services. Another middle-aged South Korean was greatly affronted in one seminar group when his critique of British democracy sparked only general hilarity. He had dismissively observed that all the citizens could look forward to was an erection every four years. He was wrong of course: it was every five years.

Democracy, Anyone?

Reference to halls of residence prompts me to say a little about the students I came across as a warden of a hall of residence, a role I happily performed for nine years. Well, to be more accurate I didn't like the first year much at all, but when I'd got the hang of it, I found this wardening business on the whole rewarding and it gave me a good overview of the student experience that frankly most academics don't get to see. Let me start by saying how strongly I agree with the Duke of Wellington: to rule men successfully you mustn't overrate them. My hall was one of six identical halls but the only all-male one. Four were mixed and the other all-female. There seemed a strong case even back then for an all-female hall: we had a significant number of Muslim girls, and others from religious backgrounds who wanted, or whose parents wanted for them, single-sex accommodation. Students coming to Hull who wished for university accommodation could apply to one hall only and since in all other respects the halls were pretty well identical, it was easy to calculate the appeal, or lack of it, of an all-male hall. Each year every hall was oversubscribed except one, the one I inherited. I discovered that ninety per cent of our inmates in my first year had applied unsuccessfully to a mixed hall in the first instance. I was sympathetic to the notion of an eventual change of status, but two events in juxtaposition convinced me to act sooner rather than later.

Early one evening, towards the end of the first term of my second year, some lads from A Block - each hall comprised five separate blocks - informed me that as they were leaving for the pub one of their number had fallen down the stairs and might have broken his arm. Off they went to the pub. I went across to A Block and found him on his bed sobbing, arm lying limp and helpless. I phoned for an ambulance and off he went to get it fixed. The second event occurred only a week or so later. One of our responsibilities as wardens was to take responsibility for all six Halls for one night each week so that other wardens could go out if they chose. The following Tuesday, my duty day, two girls from one of the mixed halls knocked on the door and reported a similar kind of event, another suspected fracture. They had sat the injured party on a chair, put a blanket round his shoulders, made him a cup of hot sweet tea and phoned for an ambulance. They just thought I should know since they planned to be going out as soon as the ambulance arrived. . There you have it: Sparta and Athens.

There and then I decided to hold a referendum the following term! There would be landslide support for a change of status: after all, the overwhelming majority were in single-sex accommodation against their wishes. Over the years since, other referendums of arguably greater significance have been held, which the proposers were as confident of winning as I was, but I had better statistical evidence to support my case than they. At the start of every term I used to print a newsletter and so in my next newsletter I explained what was to happen and added that I would be bringing out a 'referendum special' a week before the vote, and invited student contributions. In the event I received a total of approximately zero contributions, so I took it upon myself to spell out the arguments for and against in that special edition. Each student received a copy with a numbered tear-off voting slip at the bottom. A ballot box was positioned in the lobby outside our house. If anybody had wanted, they could easily have rigged the outcome but that would have taken ingenuity and energy so I was confident it wasn't going to happen. Nor did it. At 10 p.m. that evening I brought in the ballot box. Of 135 students in the hall only 65 had bothered to vote at all. Of these 31 (24 percent) had voted in favour of change and 34 (26 percent) had voted for the status quo. The people had spoken!

Then I thought: no. we *ought* to go mixed! So I put out another newsletter the following day headed: *We're Going Mixed – Only 26% Oppose!!* A short piece explained why this decision was good for the Hall and concluded that I would be happy to discuss the result with anyone. Nobody came. I felt a bit like that left-wing Miners' leader who argued against holding a ballot before striking: he wasn't going to be 'constitutionalised out of action'. But hadn't I always thought of myself as a democrat? Hadn't I taught the advantages of democracy as a form of government every year for over fifteen years? How did my intervention square with the principle of democratic participation? Well, most of the 'the people' hadn't bothered to vote at all, and of those who had, most wouldn't be in Hall the following year anyway. As for those coming in with the next intake, who would make up about 80% of the population overall, they couldn't be consulted, but history told us emphatically that a massive majority would prefer to be in a mixed hall. So did 26% of a transient population represent the "wisdom of the crowd"? Anyway, I took consolation from one of the founding members of the Fabian Society, Beatrice Webb, who had declared that she couldn't understand the theory whereby multiplying ignorant opinions indefinitely produces wisdom. We went mixed.

Cycling home one late afternoon the following November with the setting sun splashing a deep orange wash on the windows of the hall. As I approached, I heard Mozart's flute concerto in G Major floating mellifluously across the quad from C Block. On a third-floor balcony stood the flautist, the light from her room painting a halo round her head and shoulders. Quod erat demonstrandum?

The Sign of the Beast

As a warden I found that the great majority of inmates were a pleasure to be amongst. But not all. I recall a phrase in one of George Orwell's essays about the morals of some of his fellow intellectuals: he railed against their "sluttish antinomianism" .What a powerful phrase, I thought: I must find out what it means. Even without knowing though I was confident it was an appropriate description of certain of the well-to-do young gentlemen in my hall who were used to doing whatever they felt like doing, pretty well with impunity; the local branch of the Bullingdon Club. One in particular irked me, a Chemistry student, appropriately from Windsor, in his final year. One day, when I got home late from a meeting of the University Senate, where the possibility of compulsory redundancy amongst academic staff for the first time in Britain had been discussed, I found a message from the hall housekeeper telling me that overnight the door to this young gentleman's room had been smashed beyond repair. She could give me the names of five fellow thugs whom she confidently believed to have been involved in the destruction though naturally none had admitted to it. The door would have to be replaced, she went on, at a cost of £80 - about £240 today. She had set up an interview and the owner of the door was due to be arriving *chez moi* any minute. My dinner had to be put in the oven.

What riled me was the juxtaposition of these two events: the wanton destruction of expensive property in an act of what I could only call sluttish antinomianism and the unheard of threat of compulsory redundancy as the university struggled to live within its means. The only punishment open to me was to fine him, assuming he could offer no extenuating circumstances. He chose to saunter over fifteen minutes late for his appointment. offering no apology, and explained that he'd woken that morning to discover that his door had been smashed in and explained that having been drinking the evening before he'd had slept particularly deeply, so had heard nothing during the night. We are talking solid red oak here: even the excessive amount of alcohol he habitually consumed wouldn't have protected him from the sounds of such a door being trashed if he'd been a hundred yards away. Not too many adults (apart from wardens of halls of residence) could have slept through such a din. It was galling to know for certain that he knew I knew he was lying and that he assumed that there was nothing I could do about it.

He was wrong. I exceeded my powers by quite a way and told him that not only would he face a fine of £20, but the door would have to be replaced at his expense – a further £80. My advice was to undertake some detective work to see if he could possibly discover which particular miscreants had taken such liberties of a sleeping comrade. It was just possible, I added, that somebody else in the block might have heard the noise and could help him. He wouldn't have to shop anybody; I didn't need names, but did need £100 within the week, and I reminded him that University Regulations stipulated that no student in debt to the establishment could graduate. Around twenty quid each wouldn't ruin the funds of this chapter of the Bullingdon Club, but they would have significantly less to spend on sluttish antinomianism for the remaining few weeks of the term. The university got its £100 and I was chuffed. A little bit of social justice.

Each hall had five blocks and each block was built on three levels, with a small communal space on each. The set-up was not conducive to partying. The music had to be so loud it would carry to all three levels, and indeed to most of the rest of Yorkshire... Nevertheless each block had permission to hold an official party every year. I approached my first such 'block party' with some trepidation. I had appointed a Cambridge graduate who had just started on a PhD in Chemistry as my deputy; a pleasant and helpful man but not one to bang heads. On the night in question I had asked him to go over when the party was in full swing to minimise criminality. Just after 12.30 two students knocked on my door: would I come and extricate my deputy? Some partygoers from another hall had him stuck in the main door and were slowly crushing him to death. I managed to free him and took the opportunity to remind the students that block parties had to end precisely at 1a.m., i.e. ten minutes or so later. (I was certain of this rule since I'd made it up on the way over.) It worked, the noise subsided more or less on the stroke of 1 a.m. but it had been a long, long evening.

Aside from these official ones, no party was allowed without the warden's permission and mine was sought only once; for a birthday party held in A Block at 4p.m. on a Sunday afternoon when only dandelion and burdock was drunk and fish paste sandwiches, blancmange, sherry trifle and strawberry jelly were consumed. To add an impressive touch of authenticity one of the female guests was sick. Straight out of *Just William*; it must have been Violet Elizabeth Bott. I do hope she didn't get any sick on her new party frock; her mother would have been furious.

On the whole, these times were comparatively innocent. Hard drugs weren't a problem in the hall, though the housekeeper, a plain speaking old-school Scot, told me that she'd smelled cannabis on several occasions. Apparently she would threaten students in the vicinity that if she smelled it again she would have to inform the Warden. Amazingly this seemed to do the trick. Presumably they were just more careful. She told me once that she had to reprimand some students who had shifted an additional mattress into a double room. "What on earth for?" I asked. "Well, for sex... what else?" she replied blushing. "But they've already got two mattresses in there", I countered. "Aye, I know that....but *group* sex!" How come she was so well informed? What had she got up to on those dreich winter evenings in 1950s Dunfermline after the Tuesday night Young Mehtodist Social Club? Anyway, it had left her with a better grasp of the mores of this new earthly paradise than I had.

One of the downsides of the life of a Warden was the inevitability of night calls, either for fire drills or for emergencies, major and more often minor. Regarding the former, I like to think I pulled a master stroke. I managed to convince the organisers of these events that it was a waste of time their setting off the fire alarms in the middle of the night since so many of the inmates took to their beds at around 2-3 am. Far more effective if they arrived at, say, 7.30 am when they would all be fast asleep - by happy coincidence fifteen minutes after I got up in the mornings.

I had two genuine emergencies during my years and a lot more minor ones. The first of the 'real' emergencies happened one balmy summer's night. A group of our students had gone out for a drink, getting back about midnight, when some decided to sit out on their balconies to enjoy the night air. These balconies were more of a design feature than anything and comprised a low wall wide enough to stretch out on, and yet narrow enough to fall off. One returnee had elected to put both facilities to the test. Having dozed off, he suddenly found himself upside down in the rose bed eight feet below; or more accurately his mates found him. They heard the crash and the resultant groans, and came to fetch the warden. I phoned for an ambulance and in the meantime got him comfortable. I didn't want to turn him into the recovery position because I thought he might well have punctured a lung, with the noise he was making. We wardens had been obliged to take a first-aid course and so I was an expert in minor injuries. It was such a balmy night he didn't need to be kept warm so all I could do was keep him company, though all I got from him by way of contribution to the conversation was this unsettling wheeze. Soon the ambulance arrived and I offered my fellow health professionals my diagnosis: a punctured lung. Without replying, one knelt down, head close to the lad's and asked him: "Suffer from asthma, do yer lad? He wheezed an indistinct 'yeh'. I was asked to pop up to his room and find his medication. When I came back they'd sat him up and given him a glass of water. Ten minutes later after a cursory examination he'd taken his medication and was asleep in bed. Right as rain the next morning. Thank goodness for my training.

My second emergency didn't have such a happy outcome. I got a call at some time after 1 a.m. one Saturday morning towards the end of a Christmas term. A group of lads had gone into the village for a drink. Walking back just after midnight along the side of a university building one lad had chosen to vault over a set of railings, just because they were there; a harmless piece of exuberance, you'd have thought. But those railings were there for a purpose, marking off a steeply descending set of concrete steps leading to a basement door some fifteen feet down. He landed on his shoulders and head and was rushed to hospital, from where I was phoned. Would I contact the lad's family and have them come up as soon as possible? As it happened I knew the lad, knew he came from Worcester and was the only child of a widowed mother living on her own. Could I at least wait till morning before calling, I asked, explaining the circumstances? Well, no, things were looking bad. They thought she needed to be there as soon as possible. So I had to waken this poor woman in the middle of the night to give her the kind of news that every parent of an adolescent dreads: 120 miles away her only son was fighting for his life. Fortunately he pulled through, made a slow recovery and was able to come back to us the following year. However his memory was not what it had been, his powers of concentration not as acute and he had to withdraw towards the end of term and give up the idea of taking a degree.

As for minor disturbances, at the beginning of one academic year I was woken in the middle of the night by a telephone call from a Nigerian Chief whose son had newly arrived in Hall. I tolerated the first two calls, but then discovered that BST was just one hour behind Nigeria, so it had been the middle of the night in Lagos too. When a third call came I explained forcibly that I took no calls after 11 pm, and that seemed to work. His son was tall and elegant and very well dressed, so stood out in the Concrete

Tower. He happened to be a Politics student, so I kept an eye on him. When the East Riding buses altered their timetable I explained to him that he'd need to be at the bus stop ten minutes earlier to make his 9 am lectures on Tuesdays and Fridays. No problem, he assured me, he always travelled in by taxi. Towards the end of the term he came to ask me to persuade daddy to give him his book allowance in one lump sum at the beginning of the year as he only got £250. Few of my colleagues, let alone any student had so much to spend on books in a year, never mind a term. Did he need £750 all at once, I asked incredulously? Well, he didn't only spend it on books, he explained coyly, besides which, it was £250 per *month* not per term. .I told him that I was not inclined to interfere with daddy's arrangement.

Apart from the Chief's calls I recall only one other occasion when I was prized from the arms of Morpheus and it turned out to be one I didn't mind at all. About 2 a.m. one Saturday morning in May, after a fancy dress Ball on the campus, I was wakened by a ring at the doorbell. Staggering down in my dressing gown I opened the door to one of our more attractive inmates propped against the sidewall, dressed in a black bin liner, which just about managed to cover her assets, though not as comprehensively as originally. A Sunday Red Top would have paid a professional photographer a small shed load for such an image of unfeigned alluring sensuality. She leant towards me, putting her hand affectionately on my shoulder and whispered something totally incomprehensible. I feared she was about to throw up at any minute but I had to ask her to repeat her 'words', and with pretty much the same results. Then the penny dropped. "You've lost your key, right?" She must have put it in her tiny handbag – there was nowhere else available. But it was no longer there. More gurgling, but accompanied this time by a vigorous nodding and a wonderful smile. I got her a spare key, which she clasped to the top of her bin liner, "Shall you be alright?" I asked. She smiled again, raised her thumb, which I took to be a 'yes', and slid out into the night. "Sleep well" I called, "and don't forget to let me have the key back tomorrow". She pirouetted, blew me a kiss, gathered her bin liner around her and flowed off into the warm night with what sounded like "Go' Bless!"

After nine years in post we left the hall with some sadness. We wardens and warden's wives had formed strong friendships, the brotherhood and sisterhood of the trenches, and this camaraderie had added another dimension to our lives. After each term ended and the inmates had left we would hold a progressive dinner party, with a different course at each of five halls and finish with a sing song round the piano of the sixth. Our pianist being Welsh we always concluded with a rousing version of *Cym Rhonda*. The Senior Warden had a store of party games which bordered precariously on the indecent though never toppling over. These were good times. One summer we were unable to hold the dinner at the customary end of term, so organised one for the day before the students came back for the next term, though as ever some had come up a day or two early. We made such a din that the students in that hall had the temerity to complain. If there's one group that's worse than students, it's Wardens and their wives. We took away many happy memories from those years, plus a couple of fine Edinburgh crystal goblets presented by the students and a handsome painting of our hall by a well-known local artist (see front cover) which was a gift from our fellow Wardens and their wives.

The Allure of Hull

Going back some years to the late summer of my third year at Hull, I was at home alone, up a ladder, painting an exterior downstairs window frame, when the telephone rang. I should have let it ring but I was close and the door was open, so clasping the paint tin to my chest I clambered down, managed to miss my footing on the bottom rung of the ladder thereby spilling some paint, which slurped worryingly down my shirt front. On the phone was a student, a mature Scot who had come to Hull two years previously a devout Salvationist and now, less devout, was at the end of her second year. She was phoning on behalf of a friend, an African Rhodesian (Zimbabwean) trade unionist who had been forced to leave Rhodesia for political reasons and had been granted permission to stay in Britain. He was a very able man, she said, and wondered if we might interview him for a place as a mature student to start a Politics degree that autumn. (Mature students could be admitted without formal qualifications after interview.) I was

79

brief and to the point, since I could feel paint trickling inexorably down over my navel and onto my privates. Tell him to write and set out his stall. If he looks promising I will interview him. He did. I did, He came.

Three years later this charming man graduated with a good degree in Politics and Sociology and went on to become a social worker. I saw David regularly over the next dozen or so years, watched him develop into avuncular middle age. He was, I would say with confidence, at man at his ease. He would tell me, however, that happy though he was with life he retained a deep-seated ambition to return to his native land, now independent of course and safe for him. Not for good; mind, his home was now in Yorkshire, but for an extended holiday. Then one year when we met in the local grocer's he told me that his hope was to be realised: the following year he was going back for three whole Zimbabwean summer months. I asked what he was most looking forward to. Of course meeting the family was top of the list, parents, aunts and uncles not seen for twenty years, nieces and nephews never seen. But there was something specific, associated with family and friends, that he often found himself day-dreaming about in Yorkshire winters: going to the pub for a beer late on Saturday afternoons with father, uncles, brothers and friends. In singlet and khaki shorts they would walk together, barefooted, down to the pub, put the world to rights for a couple of hours before going back to a family dinner as the southern sun set. That's what he'd missed most.

And it happened - he went. I caught up with him some months after his return, in the same grocer's. How did it go? Well, he had to admit to mixed feelings. It was grand to see everyone again and to meet family members he'd never before seen, but he must have changed more than he'd realised, he continued. All those black faces everywhere unnerved him. I was gobsmacked, and disappointed for him. "But going down to the pub on Saturday afternoon, barefoot and in shorts, how good was *that*?" I asked. "Oh man, that was worst of all", he replied. "They were so parochial, so bloody right-wing. And anyway, the paving stones were baking: they burned my feet. I could hardly walk for days. I'm so glad I did it... but I'll tell you what: I couldn't wait to get back to

Yorkshire!" I haven't seen him since but I think fondly of that open face and its generous smile (I also reflect less fondly on the experience of ridding my pubic hairs of gloss paint and the sting of white spirit around the polar region.)

Teaching was most fulfilling when you found yourself dealing with a group of students who were close friends, especially if you encountered the circle in their first year and knew you'd got them for the next two years as well. Nearly always they'd motivate each other to do the reading. Class discussion would simply fly; and you would just *know* that they'd been discussing these issues in their own time during the previous week. I taught my best group in the mid Seventies. The Seventies were good years generally because you could almost count on political commitment, especially but by no means exclusively from those on the Left. There were some, it has to be said, whose commitment was so blinkered that they killed debate and antagonised their colleagues. You wondered why ever they'd come to study politics because they already knew all the answers.

I had one memorably lively group with two voluble members of the Communist Party and a fellow traveller. Both the comrades could and did come out with formulaic, even ritualistic party lines but shafts of humour would break through from time to time. I got on particularly well with one, who came from a mining village in Nottinghamshire, and held office of some kind in the CPGB. I like to think that we both enjoyed our skirmishes. About twenty years later I got a letter from him completely out of the blue. He'd always remember our class discussions with fondness, he wrote. and especially the ones on Arthur Koestler's novels *The Gladiators* and *Darkness at Noon*. I'd be pleased to hear, he went on, that in the intervening years he'd come to "see the light" and now held a senior position in a public corporation. It was good to hear from him but to be honest I wasn't pleased that he'd 'seen the light', though I was fairly confident that he wrote with more than a hint of irony. I had overheard an exchange between the comrades before we began a discussion on *Darkness at Noon*. "Did you manage to get through the book?" his mate asked. "Yeh, I did." "So what did you think?" "Well, let's put it this way. I wish I hadn't." Arthur Koestler would have been well chuffed.

Students in the Concrete Towers? I know that some academics considered them to be the only drawback to life there, but I found that being part of a community of young people at least some of whom combined enquiring minds with sharp intelligence was a wonderful way to spend one's life. I'm relieved that I taught in an age when interpersonal relations and the expression of political beliefs were regulated by good manners rather than political correctness, but I accept that things were generally less complicated then: Pandora hadn't yet opened the jar labelled identity politics. There were some students whose political bias was so strong that they were virtually unteachable, and they weren't all Politics students by any means. But not many. The longer I was in the job, the more I appreciated the pleasure of working in an environment where hope and enthusiasm were more common than resignation and cynicism.

5. *The Tower Dwellers*: *Colleagues*

Ever since leaving my home in the West Riding at the age of six or seven to go down to the East End of London with my family I've felt an outsider, and never more so than during my career in the Concrete Towers . Not that I ever woke in the morning with the deep sigh of the home-sick ex-pat, hankering after cricket on the village green or tea and toast with the Sunday papers. There was nowhere else I desperately wanted to be, nothing else I particularly wanted to do, but as an academic in the Concrete Towers I never felt 'one of us' and deep down I had an unease that one day I would be exposed . I never entertained the idea that my insecurity was a class thing and looked more to character deficiencies for an explanation. In retrospect I see the two as different sides of the same coin. I had been 'untimely ripped' from my North Country childhood security and later freely chose to become an exile from a nurturing working class family. Before the end of my first term as an undergraduate, I knew that escape was the only option for me. I didn't realise at the time that wherever I went and whatever I did I would always have baggage: being me, a permanent outsider.

"So when you gonna get a *real* job, then?" one of my Cockney cousins asked me, when he heard that I was taking up a post at the University of Hull. Fair question. Where I came from a job meant producing something tangible, or doing something that 'society' needed. For nearly all the men I had known as a child and a youth that meant working in the docks or on the river. Society also needed workers-by-brain, like doctors, managers, lawyers, and school teachers and so on, we knew that, but 'working' in a university? I'd had to explain to my mum and dad what every step on my ladder of academic progress signified, as soon as I'd got the hang of it myself of course. Like me they didn't understand about classifying undergraduate degrees, still less about postgraduate degrees and as for PhDs, well, being a doctor whose job didn't involve taking tonsils out, what was that all about? There was social kudos to be gained in those days for working-class parents, especially in a place like the Isle of Dogs where we lived, from having a child up at university, but you can overdo these things. I'd been up at university since 1959 and now it was 1967. I should be out working, settled, with a wife and family, watching West Ham every other Saturday. Thing was, I couldn't quite excise the feeling that my cousin was right: in my heart I believed that the career I was tentatively embarking on had only tenuous connections to the real world. Maybe, *maybe*, I could still fulfil my earlier vague ambition and escape into politics, after I'd established a name for myself. But in the meantime, an academic? *Qui, moi*?

In many respects, as I have explained, this world of which I felt I was not a part had already changed. I suppose that's how I got in. I've talked about the changes to universities that came with their post-Robbins Report expansion. When I was working on my Master's degree at Sheffield my supervisor made it his mission to point out to me the better prospects for those wanting a teaching position in a university. Though of course I never said this to him, I thought: who in their right mind would want to teach in a university? So when I'd got my good degree, why didn't I just take off? Ah, but there's the rub: take off where? To do what?

I sought the advice of the University's Careers Service, but apart from its imaginative proposal that I join a colonial police force, Careers were stumped when trying to discover what I was suited for. Their suggestion of the Rhodesian Police got me thinking of those lines from Burns about seeing ourselves as others see us. No disrespect to those custodians of colonial power, but was this the impression I gave to the world? On reflection though, where would I have got an appropriate role model? I knew nothing of the world of the professions. As I grew up the only future career question I put my mind to was: did I want an indoor or an outdoor job? And I never reached a conclusion even on that. I decided to wait on events, dear boy, to push me in the direction I should go. True, there was this vague idea in my mind that research could lead to a career in politics and it could have, had I bothered to pursue it energetically. To be honest I stayed on to do research for three reasons: I was flattered to be asked, there was nothing else on the horizon, and my fiancée hadn't finished her degree. So there were personal advantages to spending another year in Sheffield.

And anyway I did love History. History and Art were the only subjects in which I ever came consistently top in school and I had to give up Art at the age of fourteen. I read history books for pleasure from an early age and nobody else I knew did this. My undergraduate degree in Modern History and Government chose itself; in those days you needed an 'O' Level in Latin to read single Honours History anywhere, and I'd never taken Latin. There were only three universities where you could do History without Latin and each offered the combination Modern History and Government. But given my passion for History, why did I opt for the Politics (or Government) path for postgraduate study? Because my Government tutors asked first; had History asked first I would have jumped at the chance. I certainly didn't envisage an MA leading on to a PhD, followed by a university career. If you'd asked me at this stage what a PhD was, I couldn't have told you: I'd never heard of one. When I took up my first academic post it was the consequence of a series of serendipitous events that appear in retrospect to have had a logic to them but didn't. And after all, it was still possible to aspire to a career in politics; this was, after all, a path trodden by an increasing number of would-be politicos.

"From Hull and Halifax and Hell, Good Lord Deliver Me"

When we came back to Britain I had to get a job. Near the end of my research in New Zealand my supervisor had told me about a vacancy coming up in the Department which he and his colleagues would like me to apply for. Staying in New Zealand wasn't anything that we'd considered but anyway, as I said to him, I wasn't sure that I wanted to work in a university. His jaw dropped. "What the hell else could you do?" Had I already painted myself into a corner? Now we were back, and with limited financial resources, reality stepped in. It was April, the start of the schools' summer term. We both took teaching jobs in separate secondary modern schools, in King's Lynn as it happens, just to get a base and some earning capacity. I started to search the *Guardian* education section for university or college posts. Three possibilities came up and I pursued each: I was offered a job at what was then Bournemouth College (now University) and at Hull, and was invited to apply for a post at Bristol. Though Bristol was looking a good prospect, it wasn't a complete certainty whereas Hull was. I preferred it to Bournemouth and felt immediately at home on visiting the campus. Moreover Hull was in God's Own County and if we were to have children that meant they would be Yorkshire like their old man. And in those days boys could only play cricket for the County if they were Yorkshire born. Anyway, I wanted any boys or girls we might have to be Yorkshiremen or women.

And I certainly wasn't the only one who felt that these things mattered a lot. Amongst my undergraduate acquaintances had been a guy called John Cameron whose father, though a proud member of that clan was a Yorkshireman living in London and was much exercised that any child of his should be Yorkshire born. His wife became pregnant in 1940 as he was on the point of joining his regiment. He made provision for her to be admitted to a maternity hospital in Sheffield. She was to move north to stay with his parents in her eighth month. A few weeks later than planned she took the train from King's Cross. As the train steamed through the Nottinghamshire countryside it was strafed by a Stuka fighter-bomber and poor Mrs. Cameron began to go into labour. To his lasting chagrin John was born in Worksop. We all thought that John carried around an inferiority complex; he was always apologising for things. It was only after a couple of years into our acquaintance, and after an evening on Younger's No.3 in one of the downtown Sheffield pubs that John felt uninhibited enough to let me into the dark secret that had shaped his insecurity. Deep down, did he feel, poor guy, he'd let his dad down? No child we had would suffer that terrible fate.

So, great to be heading to God's Own, but *Hull*? I'd been there only once in my life when, as an undergraduate at Sheffield, I went east to play rugby. It was ferociously cold, that wind straight from the Steppes, and there was an unmistakable smell of fish hanging in the freezing air. As the coach came down the Anlaby Road that stench was corrosive and we all suffered. Except Bill Thompson, a towering second row forward, who could smell nothing and thought we were all pulling his leg: he was from East Hull and impervious to the charms of the fish meal factory on the other side of the Humber. Needless to say we were taken to the cleaners on that rock hard ground, and to cap it all the showers weren't working. If I never come here again, I thought, it'll be soon enough. Now we were coming to Hull to live. The auguries hadn't been great. When I drove up for interview, in the unexpected company of my father-in-law, we completely failed to find the university. Eventually I got out and asked the way. Neither of the two locals I spoke to knew where it was. I walked further on and went into a tobacconist's where I was reliably informed by a large, affable young woman in that powerful, take-no-prisoners East Riding accent that I'd been misinformed: Hull didn't have a university. Maybe I wanted the College of Commerce, she helpfully asked?

All in all then it was a pleasant surprise that when we came up flat-hunting we had no trouble in finding a well-appointed and quite elegant flat in the Avenues area, described a little unfairly as an academic ghetto: it was actually a conservation area. My wife got a job teaching on the Eastern Front and I soon got myself set up at the university and met my colleagues. What follows is an impressionistic picture of those with whom I was to work. I'm not some antique dealer showing off his favourite pieces; these were my colleagues as I saw them and probably not at all as they saw themselves. Each had or went on to a successful career. I was an outsider looking in on an unfamiliar world and for several years I felt intimidated by my new surroundings and to be honest by my new colleagues.

A Parcel of Rogues

There were ten in the Politics Department all told, including the Head. Ralph Alders reminded me of a dentist: intense, thin faced, rimless glasses, direct and frugal with words. A man you would instinctively trust with your molars. As a lad he had been involved in a cycling accident, fracturing his skull and acquiring a metal plate. He had a habit of stroking his brow when speaking, as if to hide the tell-tale dint in his forehead. When the weather was muggy the poor man would suffer from headaches. He was intent on building up his department. One of his leadership skills was the confidence to bin all mail from the university administration as a matter of course. He told me that nearly all of it was of no importance. If anything required his attention, an administrator would politely phone to see why he hadn't responded. It seemed to work and I operated a similar ploy myself much later. Ralph was a Londoner by birth and disposition and looked upon his time in Yorkshire as extended community service without the high -viz jacket and after a few years he was gone. As things turned out, we would miss his firm hand. Après lui, it turned out, came le déluge - big time.

When I considered my new colleagues at our first meeting I realised with misgivings that other than myself there appeared to be only one who seemed unsure as to what on earth he was doing there. He turned out to be the son of a Derby bookmaker, the sharpest of men, who'd arrived the year before. I mistook his initial kindnesses for tokens of friendship, but it became clear that this wasn't the case: well, it wasn't his fault he didn't take to me. On the other hand if you needed practical help, he'd be one of the men you'd turn to. For example when I laid a new concrete floor in our kitchen and asked to borrow his sledgehammer he immediately volunteered to attach his arm. He it was who offered me a piece of invaluable advice: whenever you doubt your intellectual fitness to be teaching in a university, go over to the staff common room and listen in on any conversation. You'll soon be reassured that you're one of only a few in the entire room with any common sense at all. Actually he was a bit more forthright. I tried it and it worked, and it has lasted me a life time. My other colleagues at Hull were bright, self-absorbed scholars a few of whom seemed to want to make it their business to know everybody's business including mine and preferably before I did. This did little to reassure a young man who would have doubted his mission even in the most hospitable and easy-going company.

Amongst my colleagues, I found I had most in common with Robert Nagy, a Hungarian, political philosopher. Bob's history set him apart from your average academic. He came from Budapest where he played the drums in a rock band. In the revolution of 1956 he decided to get out of Hungary with his young wife and her young daughter from a previous marriage. They slowly made their way to London where Bob, with almost no English, got a job as a porter at Harrods. They lodged with an older workmate and his wife, who befriended them.

Having acquired a command of English Bob began studying A Levels in the evenings. On the strength of two 'A's in Politics and Economics he secured a place at LSE where he subsequently graduated with a First Class Honours degree and won a scholarship to Cambridge for a PhD. Ten years after arriving in London with virtually no English, Robert Nagy had become a lecturer in Politics at a British university. Knocked my little achievements into a cocked hat.

Natural scholar though he was, Bob seemed to recognise me as a fellow proletarian and sought me out; we became and remained firm friends. We began to go out for a couple of beers from time to time. He was a soccer fanatic, and persuaded me to accompany him to Boothferry Park to watch Hull City. We would share one of the many metal stanchions towards the front of the East Stand. I would turn up about five minutes late, having secured my bike, but I could always find him. I enjoyed the games but was never able to persuade Bob to come with me to the Boulevard to watch the big boys' game, rugby league, which was becoming the chief focus of my sporting interest.

At a Departmental Meeting one summer Bob announced that he would be giving a staff seminar at the start of the autumn term on the subject of university teaching. As I've said, I was the only member of the Department who had been formally trained as a teacher and frankly I didn't want any more worthy discussions on pedagogy... *ever*... especially when delivered by a serious minded Central European. So I explained to Bob, when we were alone, why I wouldn't be attending. He laughed off my objections but I stood my ground firmly and made it as clear as I could that I wouldn't be there. Come early October Bob gave his seminar, in my absence. Apparently he delivered a *tour-de-force,* always humorous, that his audience loved...and so would I have, had I gone. Anyway, at the next home game at City I sought Bob out as usual and after a frosty greeting he said not another word during the whole game, replying to my comments with monosyllabic grunts. I put this down to the fact that City lost. But exactly the same thing next time and the next. So the following game, and we're now into December, I didn't seek him out on arrival, but went to another stanchion. At half time he came to join me and as I turned to greet him he punched me with full force in the chest. "You *bastard*", he growled, "Why didn't you come to my seminar?"

Tragically Bob died of an aneurism in his fifties, after I'd left Hull. I felt the loss of him for ages. I was asked to write his obituary for *The Guardian*. Apart from the obvious academic-y things, I drew attention to his passion for soccer and linked it to his socialist values. Supporting Hull City, I wrote, was his way of sharing in the miseries of ordinary working class life. I was later taken seriously to task for this by the local press, who were not amused by this gratuitous piece of *lèse majesté*.

Another newcomer, Alastair Duncan, an Aberdonian, was the gentlest of men, Uncle Alastair as the students called him, looked like a farmer with his checked shirts, tweed jacket, spiky, straw coloured hair, rosy cheeks, bushy eyebrows and pipe. He had a penchant for Edwardian phrases, like 'sticky dog' for when things weren't going too well; a phrase that was to come in handy when he subsequently took over as Acting Head of Department for a year and dogs got pretty sticky. His speciality was Swedish government and politics, which fitted in well at Hull, a Nordic kind of place anyway, where there was a Department of Scandinavian Studies. Alastair was content to lack oomph, content to be steady and reliable rather than spectacular. He'd written a respected textbook on Swedish politics; nothing flashy but sound and reliable. One thing you could say with certainty and this is an observation rather than a criticism, Alastair was not a leader of men, or women. Keep your chin tucked behind your shoulder and play off the front foot; no risky hooks, just drive and wait for the runs to accumulate. If more people were like him the world wouldn't be such a sod of a place. A bit duller maybe.

The fourth of the newcomers was a tallish, angular Anglo-Irishman named Declan O'Connor, who always wore a tweed waistcoat and would occasionally flourish an expensive pocket watch or Victorian snuff box as the situation required. He was seldom without a smile. His amiable disposition might have owed something to the fact that of a morning his wife, like Mrs. Morel in *Son's and Lovers*, always warmed her man's clothing for him in front of the fire. He had a passion for and a wide knowledge of classical music and towards the second year of our acquaintance persuaded me to part with £200 for a quality turntable and sound system, money that had been earmarked as the deposit for a house. My wife was thrilled. Declan was always good company especially after a drink. He might abstain for months but when the mood took him he showed a formidable capacity. He came from The Wirral where his father had a veterinary practice. I met the da' once, a down-to-earth Irishman as unlike his flamboyant son as could be imagined. His mother on the other hand was one of the most vivacious women I have met.

Declan and Robert, being both political philosophers, saw a lot of each other. Their relationship was, shall we say, complex: Declan had a genuine admiration for the Hungarian's intelligence; Robert acknowledged Declan's, but didn't admire it. In the first few years of their relationship they would sometimes go out drinking together and these sessions could last through the night. Perhaps Robert needed time and alcohol to forget that for some reason he didn't like Declan much. Perhaps he saw Declan as a threat. On one memorable session, so I was told, they drank till the pub closed and then Declan suggested they continue at the local small theatre. Since Declan sat on the management board he felt sure he could persuade them to keep the bar open for a bit. Unknown to our heroes, however, a play was being staged at the very time when they arrived. I shall set the scene as it was described to me by one of the participants.

The bar is in fact closed and nobody's around. Declan, with Robert in tow, barges through the door and straight onto the space at the front of a largish room which passes for a stage and where the action is taking place. There are at most a couple of dozen in the audience watching two characters in discussion as the drama develops when suddenly new characters appear, one of whom pretends to be inebriated. Is this Godot come at last, with his silent mate? No, as the leading character soon realises, it's Declan looking for a drink. Our thespian – it was he who told me this story - has two advantages: he has a lot of experience of local theatre and its occasional hiccups and second, he knows Declan and susses the situation immediately. With considerable aplomb he manages to steer our heroes back through the stage door promptly, as if this was just a development in the story line. A sharp word to the alarmed barman and he's back on stage. Our heroes get one drink and then are sent them packing, unaware that they had introduced a whole new dimension into that play and left a couple of dozen theatregoers pondering for days on the significance of their mysterious entry. Still, that's modern theatre!

They were even better political philosophers than drinkers and were considerable assets to the Department. There was a third much respected philosopher who had been at Hull for several years, a softly spoken Brahmin whose exquisitely structured, mellifluously presented sentences entranced student audiences. He was referred to by his colleagues as 'Sixthly' because he would always, even in private conversations, deliver his comments in numerically ordered bullet points. Like a sophisticated human power point.

The relationship between the three was always byzantine and often rebarbative. Once I overheard an absorbing discussion unfold concerning the marking of exam papers at the end of one term. There were ninety-odd scripts, each to be second-marked, so that our philosophers each first-marked thirty and second-marked another thirty. Then they met to compare and finalise the marks. Most of the students would be known to all three, so even the non-marker might have a useful contribution in deciding any disputes. They agreed nearly all the first thirty, second-marked by Bob, when he and Declan got into sharp debate on the value of one script, with Bob declaring that Declan's first mark had been over generous. "But Bob, I didn't mark it", Declan retorted "Why not?" asked Bob sharply. "Well, I didn't mark any of these" said Declan with a shrug. "I first-marked the other lot." Bob turned to Sixthly. "So *you* first-marked all the papers we've just agreed?" He insisted that they start the whole process again. All that work down the tubes and why? Because Bob had acknowledged that he had marked scripts not entirely on their merits but partly as a response to what he thought were Declan's marks. Still waters run deep.

Ralph Alders finally decided that he'd had enough of the north. A year's study leave in the United States had fuelled his discontent and he finally left us for the south west. His replacement was a strange fish; a stout, ruddy-faced Welshman with curly grey hair. He came to a department that was generally perceived to be talented but disruptive. Owen Jones was specifically appointed to better direct our talents and make us less disruptive, and one of his first actions was to fly off the handle at a junior colleague for eating an ice cream in the Department over a lunch hour. Didn't look 'the thing!' As well as making us more respectable he also had a wider, more cunning plan: to expand the Department as soon as possible. Young blood, new more malleable colleagues handpicked by himself, and not only for their good manners when handling ice cream. The University management bought the idea with the proviso that the expansion should include a second professor. Now this appointment would be out of Jones' control, so although he was promised, and got, no fewer than three new junior appointments, he also got rewarded (saddled?) with a competitor. Interestingly the two front runners for this professorial post were both former teachers of mine, though this was about the only thing they had in common. In the event a major mover-and- shaker in the profession got the job. Among the many things that Jack Halford couldn't tolerate were fools and it was into that category that he firmly placed Owen Jones from their first meeting. Jones had his skills: after all he had done remarkably well to persuade the University to expand the Department, but on the other hand he cut no figure in the profession at large. A specialist in Israeli politics, a comparative rarity, his publication record was mediocre. He later set up a small publishing house so that he could ensure that his own book was commercially published.

I'll come back to Jack shortly but first I want to say something about Michael McCann. . A couple of years after I arrived, the Department, still under the leadership of Ralph Alders, made another appointment, specifically to teach the politics of European integration. Apparently there had been few applicants for the post and only two were shortlisted. One was from Cambridge, with a number of articles in academic journals to his name and he'd wowed the interviewing panel. The other was 'just about' appointable. Fingers were crossed and breath was held, but to no avail: come the beginning of the new academic year we were joined by a young working-class Glaswegian from Nottingham University. Michael was a member of the Stalinist wing of the Labour party and was infused with political ambition. He told me later that at the age of eleven he'd had his dad take a photo of him outside No.10. His university appointment was never more than a stepping stone to greater things, and in no time at all he got himself elected to the local council where he sank himself diligently in committee work – Stalin's career path. In his university work Michael did his teaching, marked his essays and so on, but never even attempted, so far as I know, to write anything. Yet for all that he flourished.

In 1973 Britain joined the European Economic Community: suddenly European politics were the coming thing. To keep ahead of the game the University decided to create an Institute of European Studies and an appointment was made at professorial level to head this new body as Director. It was considered sensible to create an Assistant Directorship too, an internal appointment, to assist the new Director with local knowledge. Michael got the nod: there was nobody else. He hadn't managed to add to his publications record yet, but so what? He knew the ropes. He had only recently become leader of the Hull Labour party and so was a man to be reckoned with, a man with administrative competence. I happened to encounter him in the corridor immediately after his appointment. Putting his arm round my shoulder and giving me a hug, he confided: "Hey Springy my boy, meet the new Assistant Director of European Studies, who just happens to be leader of the Hull

Labour party, and still only thirty. And know what? It couldn't have happened to a nicer bloke."

But his good fortune didn't end there: The new Director stayed in post only for a couple of years and the University found it impossible to replace him immediately. So guess who was appointed Acting Director of the Institute of European Studies? And there's more, not only was McCann Labour party leader in Hull but by an extraordinary stroke of good fortune he became leader of the Humberside County Council. Humberside was a bastard creation of Edward Heath's government in 1974, which brought together two totally disparate areas which had nothing in common but the promise of a bridge over the Humber There was no love lost between the old East Riding of Yorkshire north of the Humber and the Lindsey division of Lincolnshire to the south, and the only way the Labour party, which controlled the authority, could make things work was to specify that the leadership would interchange every three years between north and south banks, in effect between Hull in the north and Grimsby/Scunthorpe in the south. McCann became the leader of the Hull party just before the end of its three years in charge, so he would become Deputy Leader of Humberside for the next three years.

At the appropriate time the party held a meeting at a local hotel to discuss who from the south should take over. Michael told me later that the night before the decision he had two visits to his room, the first from Grimsby delegates, who asked him to accept the leadership of the county, as they'd sooner someone from Hull be in charge than one of those bastards from Scunthorpe. The second visit, of course, was from the Scunthorpe delegates who also sought help from Hull to save them Grimsby. So this young Celtic hero with the flowing red locks found himself heading the Institute of European Studies and leading Humberside County Council.

Few mortals could handle such success at such a tender age and unfortunately Michael wasn't one of them. His rise was eventually more than equalled by his fall, in which not only he but also those who cared for him were badly hurt, but I don't want to follow that story. I prefer to remember Michael as a fellow working class lad whom the Fates had smiled on. Initially he simply couldn't believe his luck but before long he began to take himself seriously. By then he had no room for his old friends.

I want to leave a snapshot of Michael McCann before he fell from grace. We had a good friend who held a senior position in the World Bank and he and his wife, on a visit to the UK from Washington, came up to Hull to stay with us. We invited Michael and his young wife to dinner one evening. From the beginning these representatives of world capitalism and municipal socialism didn't hit it off, and the mutual antagonism found its most potent expression when, after eating, we played a board game called *Rat Race*. The board depicts three concentric rectangular tracks, representing the working class, the middle class and the upper class. Beginning in the outer circuit, the working class, you threw the dice and moved your piece, gaining rewards or suffering setbacks according to the square you landed on. The object was to progress through the social classes, gaining wealth and status symbols on the way. Obviously the sooner you accrued enough capital and status to rise into the middle class the better, and likewise the upper class: the circuits were shorter and the rewards (and pitfalls) more plentiful. The winner was the first to amass a fortune of £100,000 and gain three upper class status symbols Things were more complex than I'm letting on, but you get the general picture.

So here we were, playing *Rat Race* with a senior World Banker and the leader of a large English county council. Their ideological dispositions only became an issue when Michael, having amassed the necessary capital and acquired the necessary class status symbols, simply refused to move into the middle-class. He had no intention, he said, of betraying his heritage. The banker accused him of cheating! I'm not confident we had a complete set of rules, but those we had were scrutinised. Nowhere was it specified that you were *obliged* to move class. But why specify the obvious? Our scion of capital shifted tack: his class enemy was traducing the 'spirit of the game'. Meanwhile Michael continued steadily to build his fortune and to acquire middle-class status symbols. The two men nearly came to blows when Michael having amassed the necessary capital, started to acquire upper-class status symbols...whilst still moving along the outer, working-class circuit. And he won!. He could have raced rats every night for the next decade and never manage that feat again. Furious our World Banker stomped off to bed without a word. All along Michael had just been winding him up, but World Bankers don't really do irony.

Decent man that he was, Washington was full of remorse next morning, though he remained adamant that Michael's behaviour had been indefensible. We who had watched the battle from the safety of the middle class had been memorably entertained. From the perspective of the future, though, that evening came to be seen as a portent. Michael had flouted the rules, been outrageously lucky – and won. Early success notwithstanding, in real life things just didn't work out like that.

Backtrack to Jack, our newly recruited professor, whose field was French politics and government, a man whose scholarship enjoyed international recognition and who as the acknowledged leader of the Young Turks in the profession, had recently engineered something of a coup in the national association. So in our rather small world, Jack was a cheese of substantial dimensions. He drove himself single-mindedly to advance the cause of 'political science' and as is often the case with driven men, drove everyone else too. I admired and respected Jack but he could be a pain in the bum at times.

He was a great wine aficionado and one term, when he was Head of Department, he entertained an eminent French political scientist who happened to be an even more serious viniculturalist. Eminent though he doubtless was the man was, unlike his host, easy to talk to and good company. Nevertheless Jack's anxiety about getting the 'right' wine for his guest for the evening meal *en famille* was palpable. The next day we asked how it had all gone: had his guest been impressed with the wine? Well, Jack's wife had served their two young children Tizer and this amber nectar had intrigued the guest, who had asked if he might try some. He proceeded to drink nothing else all evening, declaring. "Que c'est formidable, ce Tizeur!" Jack was mortified.

Rather like Bernard Shaw and Sidney Webb and other early British socialists Jack saw himself as a political scientist. Trouble was, at heart he thought that's how we should all see ourselves, except maybe the philosophers. Myself, I never believed in the 'scientific' study of politics, except in the Aristotelian sense. Jack was tolerant of recusants like me whose work he appreciated, if only up to a point; but amongst the tolerated Owen Jones' name was not included. For the next few years they *just about* tolerated each other and took it in turns to act as Head of Department.

The Big Squeeze

In the early 'eighties, during the reign of Owen, the gaze of the Snow Queen fell upon universities: Thatcher decided that reform was necessary. And why not? Everything else had been reformed, apart of course from a political system that was dysfunctional enough to have allowed this accidentally elected party leader to run the country. Universities had their strengths, she recognised: principally scientific research, medicine, the law, management sciences. Traditional subjects like History and Modern Languages could be tolerated as necessary evils. But what about the wild frontiers of academic study? Sociology, Politics, Anthropology, American Studies? *Media Studies*? She lumped them into one category: Parasitic Studies. All you needed to do was to put the squeeze on university finances and they would give up these subjects as extravagances, wouldn't they? But this Bonfire of the Extravagancies was entirely misconceived. University income was largely derived from student numbers and guess which subjects attracted most students and which, coincidentally, were the cheapest to run? Around the country, but especially amongst the smaller and newer universities it was Chemistry departments, Physics and Applied Physics departments that were most affected, several closing. Almost every university was obliged to devise a plan to manage the constraints of Thatcher's new world.

The response of the management at Hull was creepily Machiavellian: let the troops plan the cuts themselves. Give them ownership of the butchery. That's how democracies work. So in Hull every Department was required to produce a plan, which would identify its 'strengths' and show how it proposed to protect and build on these strengths in the coming years of austerity. Jones, Head of Department at the time, called us all together to give notification that he was preparing such a plan. The crucial consideration now should have been: what does Jack think? But Jack was on study leave and was utterly determined not to ruin it by getting involved.

By this time I was a Senior Lecturer and had accumulated considerable administrative experience, one way or another. I argued against drawing up any such plan because what it would really identify was our weaknesses, not our strengths; areas, meaning individuals, not central to the departmental 'profile' and so expendable. It was as if we had been informed that some of us were to be gassed for the common good and now our executioners were asking us to lend them 50p for the meter. No: let them do their own dirty work. That's what I said. Most of my colleagues felt the same. Jones told me, resignedly, that I was being too negative: we should *celebrate* our strengths and show that the Department didn't have any weaknesses. He would illustrate this by drawing up a plan which we could all study at leisure prior to another meeting to be held a week later. Sounded fair enough at the time, but come Thursday, the day before the proposed meeting, the odour of deceased rodent was detectable: no plan had been circulated, an old management tactic. We would have the promised document but with no time to scrutinise it. Sure enough, it arrived in the internal post after lunch on Friday, the day of the meeting – and it only confirmed our misgivings.

It seemed that our great strengths were political philosophy and European politics. The latter included the UK, an area in which four of us worked, Italy (one colleague) and France (Jack), the EC itself (one colleague, the European Woman of the Year no less). Interestingly the concept of Europe stretched all the way to Jerusalem: Well, why not? It did in Roman times and come to think of it Israel had an entry in the

Eurovision Song Contest. But our European specialisms apparently didn't include Sweden, Abba and *Waterloo* notwithstanding. Alastair Duncan's research wasn't recognised in the plan as part of our 'strength'. There were other anomalies but this one caused an eruption at the subsequent meeting and Jones felt obliged to close it within ten minutes. Three days later, out of the blue, he resigned and to coin a phrase we never saw him again. I didn't like Jones but it would be churlish to overlook the difficulties he faced or ignore the fact that the Department's earlier expansion was in good part his doing. Its subsequent rise to some national eminence, though greatly enhanced by Jack's leadership, was also based upon the work of the young cohort that Jones' managerial skills did much to create and encourage.

I can't let Owen go without telling of The Jones Formula. He had dispensed with the services of one young secretary with disarmingly pert breasts whom he'd found once after office hours *in flagrante*. Jones had been genuinely shaken and at a subsequent departmental meeting he spoke sincerely about the problems associated with appointing a replacement. At great length he explained why it wasn't a good idea to appoint a *young* female as secretary. However wide her range of office skills: she would be too vulnerable to the wiles of students. On the other hand a very *attractive* secretary, whatever her organisational abilities, might inadvertently, or indeed advertently, arouse younger members of staff. Finally, and counter-intuitively he acknowledged, it didn't do to appoint someone who was manifestly *efficient* because as soon as they'd learned the ropes they would be poached by a larger department. These considerations, he explained, would shape his approach to the next secretarial appointments. At the end of this rambling articulation of strategies I asked if it might be useful to summarise his ideas into what we might call the Jones Formula for Appointments. What we should be looking for was a candidate who was old, ugly and inefficient. I don't think my summary endeared me to him but to be fair to Jones, it might have made an impact because he went on to appoint a young, vivacious and exceptionally efficient woman who revolutionised office procedures and proved to be only the first in a string of glittering later secretarial appointments.

New Kids on the Block

Of the four young colleagues appointed during Jones' expansion, each went on to obtain a Chair and become a Head of Department. That's not a bad reflection on the quality of the Department at Hull. They were a disparate quartet. One was prematurely bald with a cone-shaped head, inevitably nicknamed The Mekon by the students, with whom he was always popular. He was a closet gay at the time but came out when 'out' was rather fashionable, only subsequently seemed to go partly back in again. He loved himself to bits, a sentiment never to become contagious amongst his colleagues, though I found him a pleasant enough colleague. He acquired a formidable knowledge of constitutional law and practice on which he would build, through a mixture of a lot of hard work, flagrant self-publicity and the right connections, a very successful career. What he lacked however was the power of imagination. We were given a fascinating seminar on graphology by a psychologist from Leeds one Wednesday, after our new colleagues had got their feet under the table. The psychologist showed us some amazing examples of well-known monikers, Charles Dickens and Adolf Hitler come to mind, to illustrate how signatures might offer a key to understanding character. Truly creative individuals, he went on, almost invariably had ornate, often indecipherable signatures. Hitherto our man's signature had been almost child-like in its rounded simplicity; a nursery window looking in on a soul entirely contented with itself. Overnight his signature transformed itself into an impatient gash, an angry stroke of the pen which was as utterly undecipherable as it was designed to be. And the next day his imaginative powers began to multiply prodigiously. He went on to achieve his life's ambition and park his bum on the plush red benches of the House of Lords.

Our second new colleague was a mercurial Mancunian with a sharp mind. When we were on a hill walk once he told me about an incident from his youth when, as I remember it, he'd been instrumental in securing the safety of a school group lost on some murky Lake District fell. He had discovered himself to be a man to turn to in a crisis. We need such men. The downside was that our colleague tended to portray

101

every problem as an impending crisis requiring hard decisions and decisive action, under his leadership, especially if it might involve knocking heads together. Cometh the hour cometh the man, and if the hour faileth to come, hustle it along a bit. Show you've got the balls. "So dauntless in war, there never was knight like the young Lochinvar". Most of his older colleagues found this rather exhausting. But the real Lochinvar had been a winner and our colleague too went on to enjoy a very successful career.

The third colleague's specialism was in the politics of the EU. She came with the impressive title of European Woman of the Year, an accolade which, since the year in question was specified, would naturally begin to lose some of its lustre as time passed. A gastro-pub I frequented up by Pitlochry sported a poster declaring it to have been Scotland's *Pub of the Year* in1871. You did find yourself wondering about the condition of the pickled eggs. She was able, overweeningly ambitious and well 'networked' a word I'd never encountered before meeting her. If there is such a thing as a collaboration gene the angels must have been out of stock when she came into the world. She focussed on her career and didn't put herself out for others who, in turn, didn't put themselves out for her.

In these pre-email days peremptory messages to colleagues had to be sent through the internal post, as a memo. She was the queen of the peremptory memo and would cascade them even onto colleagues with rooms down her corridor. This would piss them off especially if, as was usually the case, she was asking a favour. As Head of Department I had formally to appraise her. She told me how unhelpful colleagues were; they resented her as a successful woman. I have no doubt she would have encountered prejudice and would have had to learn to fight her corner, but I put it to her that it might have been her peremptory style as well as her gender and success that colleagues objected to. She might do better to speak to colleagues personally rather than send them memos, especially if she were asking a favour. We had both to sign a document agreeing a plan of action: it stated that she would dispense *altogether* with memos to departmental colleagues. In the event no change in her behaviour was discernible. When little brown envelopes with her unmistakable handwriting turned up in my pigeon hole they always contained *two* memos, one explaining why it had been reluctantly necessary to send the second. But none of this stopped her from eventually getting a chair in another Yorkshire university.

Finally the fourth new colleague. He was as just able as the others, but less overtly ambitious. A family man, tolerant, with a pleasing, dry sense of humour. A product of Ushaw College, the seminary in County Durham, he had trained for the priesthood but had lost the calling and eventually joined the administrative class of the civil service. Trainee priests leave to become hippies or rock stars or just drop- outs, but a civil servant? He hadn't so much forsaken the privations of monastic life as swapped monasteries. He was a man of many attributes but carried himself as if God had marked him out, Job-like, for suffering. Not surprising, I suppose, since he'd been born into a family of Tranmere Rovers supporters. His area of research was Italian politics, a subject that never sat still long enough for the artist to manage a decent portrait. Like Sisyphus and his rock each time our colleague had neared completion of a detailed analysis of the Italian governmental system, there would be some seismic event that shook everything up and he'd have to start again. His ascent of the greasy pole turned out to be a tougher proposition than it would be for his contemporaries but he deserved to make it and he made it.

Personally I got on well with each of these new colleagues, but have to say that I found them single-mindedly ambitious in a way unlike most of us more established academics, more individually competitive, more careers focused. And they deeply despised each other.

This wasn't supposed to be a comprehensive list of colleagues at Hull, but I will mention one more. Politics was joined at the hip to South East Asian Studies, with two, sometimes three academics lecturing in the politics of that region. One of these could have been created by the *Telegraph* cartoonist Matt. Christopher – *never* Chris - was, in nearly all respects but personal wealth, a man of substance. Heavy jowelled, his face gave the impression of a man whom someone has attempted to strangle but been interrupted. He held his head unusually straight, what hair he had grew upwards and his eyes bulged. The son of a missionary, he had spent his early years in a Japanese prison camp and after the war his family had moved to New Zealand, though even from a distance he was quintessentially, unmistakably English. Had there been any lingering doubt on the matter, after the death of an uncle he began to appear in an inherited tweed shooting jacket and plus fours. He drove a Jaguar at least one hundred and fifty years old at a steady forty-five miles an hour from a small village near Malton, always arriving ten minutes late for his 9 am tutorial clasping his' breakfast', a carton of coffee and a cheese roll, which he would proceed to dunk into the coffee and consume whilst teaching. He intrigued the students, especially since he insisted on lecturing in front of a pre-war wall map showing a world that was predominantly pink. Regularly challenged on this by his students, his justification, that he thought the world had been a better place when mostly pink, seemed to disarm them. Maybe some secretly agreed with him but most just realised the futility of discussion: Christopher came from a place a long, long way away.

Christopher and I kept in touch after we had both left Hull, he to work in a private university in Turkey, me to go north to Scotland. On his retirement he moved to live by one of the Italian lakes – he was fluent in Italian of course - and subsequently told us in one of his regular Christmas letters that on his 80th birthday a few months before, he'd successfully attempted some prestigious lake swim "in the buff, don't you know?". Of course, Christopher, how else?

Star of the "Stirling Shopper"

I'd no idea that when I accepted the Chair of Political Studies at the University of Stirling in 1991 I would became a celebrity overnight throughout Stirlingshire and parts of Clackmannanshire, or at least among those discerning locals in these counties who read the relevant edition of the *Stirling Shopper*. My picture appeared in amongst the adverts offering bath oils and beans, along with a brief paragraph explaining who I was, under the heading 'New Challenge for Tom'. Some have greatness thrust upon them.

I had been 'tasked', as they say nowadays, by my new employers with re-establishing a department that had been officially disbanded five or six years earlier. Three colleagues were still teaching Politics courses to the small number of students who had embarked on Politics degrees while the Department was still a going concern and who, for one reason or another, hadn't yet completed, as well as students from other Arts and Humanities departments. When the Politics students had completed their degrees the Department was to melt away. But a new Principal had decided to resurrect the discipline and to re-establish a small Department which might, if successful in attracting students, develop a teaching establishment of six or maybe even eight, a reasonable size for a small university. So my first task would be to win the confidence of my three colleagues in the future of the Department and make a number of new appointments over a few years. This was what had attracted me to the job: to be building something up when many of the structures of Concrete Towerland were being torn down to save money

I was given a remit by the appointing committee to build a European focus into the teaching and research programme, since Europe was The Future. So our first new appointment would be a 'Europeanist' and we were delighted with the strength of the field of applicants. The Principal chaired that appointing committee and on an early spring afternoon we met in a bright, airy room with views out over the loch. All was well with the world. We sat waiting for the first applicant, due at 2 pm. When by 2.10 there had been no discreet knock on the door the Principal peevishly instructed me to go down stairs, locate the applicant, a young American woman, and fetch her up forthwith. Chop-chop. So down I went to the find the porter. "Applicants for interview for the post in Political Studies?" I enquired with a winning smile. "Ay, laddie, set yersel' doon ovver there. They'll call ye when they want ye." Hadn't this man seen the *Stirling Shopper*? We appointed that woman and she proved to be not only an excellent teacher and stalwart colleague, but a ray of Californian sunshine. We grew eventually to eight: four sober British males, two young American women, a German woman and a young French woman. It was an excellent department and, I think, a happy one. And we did some innovative things: we joined a summer teaching programme, ran a part-time degree, and created a fluid structure that would allow students to transfer into the second year of our four-year degree course from local further education colleges. In the company of these colleagues I enjoyed the best ten or so years of my career and I believe that the students who studied with us in those years had as rich an experience as the limited resources of our particular Concrete Tower could provide.

Our young French colleague came from a culture significantly different from our own. I was in the departmental office once, after she'd been with us for a month or two, when she came in with an armful of books. She put them on a sideboard and asked the secretary in a rather peremptory way to take them over to the library, on the other side of the campus, since she'd finished with them. The look she got must have come close to immolating her: was this the face that sank a thousand ships? The books stayed on the sideboard for a week or two before our young colleague managed somehow to get them all the way over to the library entirely by herself. This attitude made her unpopular with the students. She showed me a written threat of physical harm on the day before she was due to invigilate the final examination of her course for mature students in the evening degree programme. That was when the would-be assailant had threatened to strike.

Although I took it to be some kind of prank she was visibly shaken and I offered to take the invigilation for her. She refused point blank. I felt it my duty to inform the administration but made it clear that she had insisted on carrying out the invigilation. I also mentioned it to my senior colleagues. That evening three of us, acting independently, accidentally bumped into each other whilst patrolling the corridor outside the examination room: me, a senior colleague and a senior member of the administration. We were all a little embarrassed. Nothing happened, but we admired this young woman's refusal to be intimidated by older men. Our Gallic colleague left us after four years for the Institute of Political Science in Paris, but not before taking the prize for the young French Political Scientist of the year.

From the beginning at Stirling I tried to build a sense of community, something that hadn't characterised the Hull department. We used to take off for an 'away day' each summer, to an inn on the banks of Loch Earn, where we would spend two days and one night. We had the use of the library for our meetings during the days, punctuated by coffee and scones, and would enjoy a decent meal in the evening followed by an hour or two in the bar. My successor as Head of Department decided this was an unnecessary expense and substituted a modest non-residential day event in its place. I think the Department lost something important in the process. But quite independently of this change other, unavoidable changes occurred: some of my colleagues moved on, one whose company I had particularly enjoyed retired. Then a few years later I retired too.

I will always be grateful to the Gods for that decade, not only the happiest of my academic life but also the most productive. This, I thought, was what academic life in the Arts and Humanities was all about. Or should be.

6. *The Tower Dwellers: Administrators*

How many heterosexual men north of middle-age can honestly say they didn't lust after the leather clad Emma Peel from *The Avengers* back in the Sixties? When I heard that Dame Diana Rigg, who played the delectable Emma was to become the new Chancellor of my university, Stirling, images of a vibrant Mrs Peel turning out in her leathers for the Graduation Ceremony flooded my imagination. Naturally I knew that she had to be in her sixties by then so the likelihood of her doing so wasn't too great. But dreaming is for free. Through her marriage she had spent time in the Stirling area and once, by chance, the previous Christmas, I'd found myself standing next to the Dame at the check-out at the local Woolworth's. And there are not many men north of middle age who can claim that. Anyway, in her ten-year term of office she was often to be seen around the campus, though never in her leathers. On one Graduation Day when we members of staff were lining up in our academic gowns ready to process through the hall and onto the stage for the annual Degree Congregation I found myself, once again, standing alongside Mrs Peel. We were in a corridor, waiting for our cue, behind a swing door that led into the back of the hall. She pushed the door open, took a good look inside, pulled the door to, turned to us and proclaimed dramatically: "It's a full house darlings." I mention this not merely to show that I have moved in exalted circles but to start my description of university administration right at the top, with the Chancellor.

The Boss in Focus

Although the Chancellor is nominally Head of the University, they are symbolic figures bringing principally public visibility. Some are more active than others. If a student body had some grievance against their institution it's possible that a Chancellor might become involved but, like a constitutional monarch, they would need to be wary. Diana Rigg, I believe was more active than most, and as was appropriate, kept good contact with the Film and Media Studies Department at Stirling.

So if the Chancellor doesn't run the show, who does? Not surprisingly it's the Vice Chancellor, or Principal in Scotland, with the assistance of several Pro-Vice Chancellors or Deputy Principals. Most Vice Chancellors have a successful academic career behind them but at some stage, as that career advanced, they have become increasingly involved in the running of their institution and one thing has led to another, and finally they have felt qualified to become the boss, though usually they apply for the top job in another establishment. What makes for a successful Vice Chancellor? The respect of one's colleagues is a good guide, but that's not always easy to gain, especially if one has swapped institutions. One of the Vice Chancellors under whom I worked gave me an insight into what problems the new person faces on arrival. Unless they have been appointed with an agreed programme, almost always involving cost-cutting, they will want to make as few changes as possible until they are well established. However they are likely to come to an institution riven by factions, because most of them are, each looking to the new leader to sort their opponents out at the earliest opportunity. Inaction isn't an option. You decide what has to be done as a matter of urgency and you do it. Eighty percent of your colleagues support your action, twenty percent are opposed. But that's a result, right? Think again. That eighty percent won't be strongly supportive, because after all, you only did what *had* to be done. The twenty per cent who were opposed, on the other hand, now completely despise you. The next year you take another, similar necessary step, and again, eighty percent are supportive, twenty percent fiercely opposed. But not the same twenty percent as last year. And the same again the following year, with similar results. Within three years you might have improved the way the university operates, perhaps even substantially, but the majority of your colleagues hate you. Thereafter you are thinking more about survival than anything else. Vice-Chancelloring? Hardest game in the world.

Administrative competence is a commodity that institutions hug close to their bosoms; it's a comparative rarity. I became involved in administration myself and indeed in mid-career had to make an assessment of what I wanted from the rest of my academic life: to roll back on my purely academic commitments and turn to administrative responsibilities or to turn my back on these responsibilities and anchor myself in research and teaching. Some fudge was probably inevitable, but I had to make my mind up about what my priorities were. When push unavoidably came to shove I had no hesitation in choosing to be an academic and not an administrator, though I couldn't avoid becoming the Sub-Dean of a Faculty towards the end of my career at Stirling.

President Franklyn Roosevelt is supposed to have declined to appoint academics recommended to him for advisory positions in his administration because whenever he turned to them their response would always be: well, on the one hand such-and-such but on the other hand such-and-such. Men and women of action can't be doing with prevarication. As a matter of fact, in all my dealings with other universities I found that that they were all generally badly managed. I was surprised how often colleagues in other universities would take it for granted that I'd heard all about how badly their particular institution was run; they seemed to think that it was a byword for maladministration and incompetence. Not so, to varying degrees they were all mismanaged, but the institutions of those days were far smaller and consumed far less of the public purse than is the case today. It didn't matter so much.

Putting the Clocks Forward

In my early years at Hull, somebody had the bright idea that the teaching day should be 'rationalised'. At the time teaching in the mornings began on the hour, starting at 9am, but in the afternoons it began at quarter past the hour, starting at 2.15. There had originally been a reason for this – something to do with bus timetables I believe – but nobody seemed to remember the details and anyway those extra fifteen minutes at lunchtime were welcome. The discrepancy offended the administrative mind however and became a subject for lengthy discussion at Senate... several times. At last a committee was appointed. It deliberated for six months: should the afternoon sessions be brought in line with the morning's or vice versa? At the end the 'on-the-hourists' and the 'quarter-pastists' were as far apart as ever... well, about 15 minutes actually. So they decided on a compromise:

afternoon teaching would henceforth begin not on the hour, nor quarter past the hour either, but... at 10 minutes past the hour. You think I'm making this up? There's a ditty in *My Fair Lady* that concludes: "So rather than do either/they did something else that neither/liked at all."

Even so there is a virtue to this way of doing things: it promotes civilised exchange. True the end results often represent cock-ups, but usually not many people die. The committee that produced the time-table cock-up would have met during lunch breaks, been provided with coffee, biscuits and the spirit of compromise. It took six months to achieve a laughable outcome but at least that allowed time for prisoners to be exchanged.

As universities expanded resource and financial management became increasingly important and universities would often look beyond academia for their senior leaders. Businessmen and women with successful careers behind them became more common in senior administrative positions. And they didn't come cheap. Moreover Polytechnics had always been run more or less as businesses and when in the 1980s they became universities they brought their business models with them and some traditional universities adopted some of their practices. So for example Deans running Faculties or Schools became permanent administrators rather than academics persuaded to take 'Buggins' turn' for three years. This development had the effect in many but not all institutions of creating hostility between academic staff and administrative staff. I never doubted that there were able administrators who tried to serve the interests of their institution, but on a number of important issues I found that I didn't share their perspective. I shall have more to say about this later.

Budding Young Administrator

Soon after I began my academic career I found myself in the role of a university administrator, in a small way you understand, when I was made responsible for ensuring that my department made the right number of offers at the appropriate level to meet the student target numbers for our various courses. Since funding followed student numbers it was important to fill all places. On the other hand, if you exceeded targets you would have to do more teaching with no extra resources. In some years the government would financially penalise any university that over-recruited and the departments responsible would lose funds accordingly; in other years governments would demand that universities increase their targets, so it would be necessary to go out into the highways and byways of the larger northern cities and drag in any idle young person seen loitering about. From year to year you could never be sure which of these policies, or something in between, the government would opt for, which made a lottery of all attempts at forward planning. I played this lottery in conjunction with my immediate 'boss', the Faculty Admissions Officer.

I made it my business to go over to his office for a chat, to get his advice on how to go about my responsibilities. I discovered that. even discounting the vagaries of government policies admissions constituted a dramatic landscape full of known unknowns, with unknown unknowns lurking behind every rock, the biggest and most threatening of the known unknowns being that most offers by far were conditional on 'A' level results, and as we've seen., funny things can happen with 'A' Level results. To my amazement I discovered that the Faculty Admissions Officers, despite their expertise, didn't have the authority to require me as a departmental tutor to adapt my departmental strategy; they could only advise. Supposing, as sometimes happened, the years' examination cohort performed less well than expected. The departmental tutor might decide to accept students who had fallen one point below their original offer, so BBC becomes BCC. In my second year as admissions tutor, I was in the Faculty office in August when the tutor for Law stomped in. Early Law results from the first Board to declare, the Welsh A Level board, were looking bad, he said, and he wanted to lower all offers with immediate effect. Wait, the Faculty Officer advised; maybe the Welsh Board's out of line. No, the Law tutor was adamant; he had to act swiftly and decisively. Places would be offered to all who came within one point of their original offer. The Law target overall was 70: that year Law recruited 104 students. For the next three years Law colleagues had to teach 50% more students with no additional resources.

In my third year at Hull I myself was elevated to Faculty Admissions Officer for three years; unpaid of course. I spent two half-days per week in the Faculty Office over the year but had to be in around the clock for two to three weeks from mid-August. I found it alarming how little departmental admissions tutors knew about the standards of the various Boards or about overseas and international qualifications. They would come to me for advice, senior academics some of them – *me*, who had been at the university all of two years. Happily I did know something about the various qualifications and so could offer advice. These experiences taught me that most academics, even the successful ones –especially the successful ones - aren't generally cut out for administration.

Travelling Salesman

Some years further down the line, after I became a Senior Lecturer, I was asked to chair the University's Schools Liaison Committee which oversaw the crucially important operations and funding of the university's recruitment policy. I got to know those who worked in that service, professional administrators all, though naturally all had degrees. These recruiters knew far more about most aspects of the university's teaching programmes, its sporting and social facilities, the international standing of its various departments and individual scholars, its accommodation policies, almost everything about the university, than anyone else with the possible exception of some Vice Chancellors. Most of them spent their time going round the country, some around the world, attending 'fairs' in which they would sit in a large hall behind an appropriately festooned desk along with the representatives of many other institutions and field enquiries from would-be applicants from local schools. Sometimes they would visit individual schools. They were, in effect, travelling salespeople.

At one meeting of the committee, the senior Schools Liaison Officer pointed out that although I made recommendations to Senate about

114

policy and funding I'd never been to a recruitment fair to see what it was all about. Well, I agreed to make myself available to go on a visit the following month. They sent me to a fair in darkest Wigan! And to tell the truth I quite enjoyed it. Would I go again, he asked? Maybe, I replied, but only once in a way; I wasn't blessed with time. One November afternoon when I was working from home, the Schools Liaison senior officer phoned to ask how my diary was looking for the following March. I immediately thought: Preston? Oldham? Accrington? Unfortunately, I lied, my diary was at work - why? Well, he explained, a senior recruiter from Heriot Watt University was organising a recruitment trip around Europe which would take two weeks, starting in Brussels and going on through six European countries and finishing in Lisbon. They would visit British schools in these cities hoping to recruit European but especially international students with a background in the English education system.

Whereas British students brought no fees with them in those days, international students brought about £3000 per annum. The trip would certainly prove expensive, but would it be worthwhile? Richard wasn't sure. "We have to cover it though: it could be a big earner. None of us in the Office can make it and we hoped you might be able to: it's the last week of the Spring Term and the first of the Easter holidays." Well, I'm thinking, nothing much happens in that last week of term, so I could make it...and it sounded a little more exciting than industrial Lancashire. "Hang on, here we are", I replied, "I do seem to have my diary after all...now, let's have a look...what were the dates? Hm...I reckon that should be OK... with a bit of juggling...."

It turned out to be hard graft but most enjoyable. We were well catered for and the mission was a considerable success for Hull. So I went again: five times. We didn't always go to the same schools or countries, so I saw quite a few European capitals. Though hard work - on one admittedly exceptional day we breakfasted in Vienna, had lunch in Milan and dinner in the Swiss Alps, doing some business in each country - these visits were full of pleasant experiences and we usually had a weekend free, so we did get to see something of some of Europe's more beautiful cities.

We would usually attract say a couple of hundred students on our visits, which always followed the same pattern. In an opening plenary session our leader would explain the working of British Higher Education, then each of us would speak for two minutes backed by a slide of our own institution. Each of us would adopt a personal strategy in our little talks at the beginning. Mine would always be wrapped around a joke. The students didn't come expecting to laugh and I hoped it would make them think of coming to see me. After these mini-talks we would break and each of us would occupy a desk replete with university literature, and students would speak to us individually. Each year I recruited numbers of overseas as well as European students, repaying the University's investment many times over.

It wasn't so easy to sell Hull in southern Europe where the UK was believed to stretch from London to Oxbridge. In Milan one spring, for example, I endured a dire afternoon when only a handful of students visited my table. At the end of this purgatory our leader announced that we'd all been invited to dinner at the home of the Chairman of the School Governors out at Monza. "Best Bib and Tucker job, I'm afraid", he concluded. This was the last thing I wanted. I'd been feeling increasingly Yorkshire and working-class all afternoon amongst these well-heeled, über sophisticated young people. I wanted a quiet meal and a beer or two.

At Monza the Chairman's magnificent apartment was in the former Austrian Embassy, which for no good reason raised my hackles further. When we were individually introduced to the Chairman's decorous wife, a middle-aged blonde in a tight black dress, I was overcome by a powerful vision from Lindsay Anderson's *If* of Malcolm MacDowell on the chapel roof with a machine gun shooting all the parents at Speech Day. "And this is Dr. Tom Spring from Hull," said our leader. Her whole demeanour changed. She gave me a big hug. It seems they'd lived in the region for seven years and planned to retire to a Wolds village. She loved Hull and the East Riding. The whole evening was spent in her delightful company and we had a lot of laughs. Thank goodness I'd left the machine gun back at the hotel.

There was another side to overseas recruitment which was altogether darker: the unseemly competition to attract overseas students, more precisely their fee incomes, by lowering entry requirements. Some universities regularly admitted overseas students with the kind of grades that would have debarred any British student. This is not only perniciously unfair but does a disservice to a weak student who might well find the course too demanding and perhaps even fail their degree. This practice was immoral and unwholesome to observe. And I saw it happen often enough, especially at post-graduate fairs; but never, cross my-heart-and-hope-to-die, on our tours.

We were a motley bunch, with only a few full-time active academics like me. I don't think I would have survived the wear and tear of doing the job on a daily basis as most of them did, but I did enjoy the occasion venture, and not only to foreign parts. I loved my trips to Orkney and Shetland, once being blessed with a memorable sighting of the Northern Lights from the low hills north of Lerwick, where I'd been driven by a member of staff. I went to Belfast on four or five occasions for example and to Derry, Newry and Coleraine too. Call me biased, since one side of my family came originally from County Antrim, but generally speaking I found the ratio of laughs per session was noticeably higher in Northern Ireland than anywhere.

Another phenomenon that I tend to associate with the North of Ireland was the occasional appearance of an odd figure hovering round my table but not coming to speak to me until the end of the session when others were leaving and I would be busily packing away posters and leaflets. They would be loners; usually boys and they would sidle up and, without looking at you directly, ask if your university had a degree course in some inevitably obscure discipline. And we usually would have, as they'd no doubt already discovered from the prospectus. Sometimes they would have excellent grades but more often their predicted grades would be well below what was needed. What to say?

Try to assure them that if they work hard, etc., or advise them to be more realistic and go for something more mainstream but less demanding? One session in Derry brought just such a young man who hung around in the background for half an hour then pounced just as I was all packed and about to leave. "Do youz do dugrees in Ombulance Draivin?" University admissions officers cry out for 'niche markets', a potential area of study that no other university has developed so they can make it their own. None has taken ownership of this particular niche. Not yet...

Recruiting in the Far East later became a major feature of most universities' programmes but I never got that far. I understand it could be quite gruelling in the steamy climates of South East Asia. One fastidious recruiter from Edinburgh told me that he would finish each day completely frazzled, and would often long to take a massage, which nearly all hotels provided. Good Presbyterian boy that he was he always resisted because massages were given in private rooms and he was apprehensive about the range of services that might be on offer. One morning in Bangkok he noticed a sign for a massage parlour and he investigated it. Sure enough there were widely spaced massage couches in rows. Safety in numbers, he thought. So that evening, after a typically gruelling day, he headed down to the changing rooms with his white dressing gown, changed and preceded to the parlour. To his dismay he found himself being quickly ushered into a side room by a charming young masseuse who asked him to lie on the couch face up, with just a towel around his privates. Then she slowly, expertly began to massage his muscles, beginning at the shoulders, and immediately he felt all his anxieties ebb inexorably away. All except one, though soon this one little niggle began to expand when those deft hands neared, but didn't quite touch, his private parts. To his dismay his towel took on a new angularity as his Presbyterian private parts slowly started to waken from what had probably been quite an extended slumber. Inevitably the young lady noticed and with a knowing smile gently laid her hand on the towel, saying, "I see that Little Brother has decided to join us. Do you think he might like a massage too?" With one bound our hero was off the couch, garbling as he grabbed his things: "No... I really don't think he would... thank you", and fled in terror. Thereafter, however stressed and sweaty, neither he nor Little Brother put massage facilities to the test again.

When finally I left Hull to take the Chair in Politics at Stirling they seemed sorry to see me leave in Schools Liaison. One of the duties the office undertook was the back-stage administration of degree ceremonies. Most of the academics who attended would hire gowns for the ceremony which would be laid out alphabetically in an anteroom. The last ceremony I attended was only a month or so before I left for Stirling and when I searched amongst the numerous 'S's' my gown was nowhere to be seen. I approached the young administrator from Schools Liaison who'd laid them out and explained my problem. "Hm" he mused thoughtfully. "Have you tried looking in the next pile, under 'T' for traitor?"

In the Vice Chancellor's house, there are many mansions...

Student recruitment was an activity that few of my colleagues undertook. Likewise student accommodation. After my experience with student houses I had decided to apply to become the warden of a hall of residence – I've already referred to this - and so to play a part in this sector of university administration too. During my years at Hull the University owned and managed ten halls of residence, six of which, known as The Lawns, built in parklands in the Sixties, were designed by Gillespie, Kidd and Coia, who won an international award for them. From the university's point of view although the housing of students was an important function it was entirely subsidiary. Consequently when the Great Financial Squeeze was imposed on universities in the Thatcher years, administrators were concerned to provide this service as cheaply as reasonably possible. An awkward word, 'reasonably'.

After the Great Revolt of 1968, the student body secured representation on the committee that oversaw accommodation, and so had a small say in what was and what wasn't 'reasonable'. University administrators would try to smuggle their economies in without formal discussion in committee. But whose side were the hall wardens on? Nobody wanted the university to go bust and nobody wanted to screw the students, but inevitably specific issues produced a tendency for factions to form. For example, the administration decided it could abolish the role of housekeeper. As we've seen, housekeepers performed an essential liaison function between the students and the warden, a full-time academic after all. This issue was never formally discussed in committee, so to us wardens it was presented as a *fait accompli*. But when the manager of the halls announced the decision in committee there was such a resoundingly dismissive response from the wardens and the student reps that the idea was immediately dropped.

Another proposed economy that caused a furore came like a bombshell at the end of an informal clear-the-air evening get-together between the wardens and a senior administrator over a pint or two. As the evening closed and he was literally half-way out of the door he turned and he said as an aside, "Oh, one other thing. You might turn your minds to how you're going to cope when you have to run two halls instead of just one." This scheme wouldn't have saved any money since wardens weren't paid, they just got free accommodation. A few extra rooms - without balconies - constituted the only saving. Universities didn't choose such tight budgets but the efficient and economical running of the system required our goodwill and this piece of amateurish Machiavellianism was scarcely the best way to achieve it. Once again, our case was conceded.

Have Expertise, Will Travel

Fast forwarding towards the end of my career, when I began to find my administrative experience sought out by several universities who asked me to undertake an informal review of the work in their Politics Departments. By this time I had acquired enough forensic ability to make a contribution to the work of those departments and was happy to agree. Fortunately I was never asked to visit a Department I didn't respect. My final administrative role, though, was undertaken when I'd officially retired but was still teaching at the Politics Department at

Stirling. I was invited to advise a university in Eastern Europe on how to adapt its provision of Politics to European standards. I visited them twice a year for a week a time over a period of five years. The institution I had to assist in reforming was called an Institute of Politology which, as the name suggests, was still largely a Soviet-style institution and operating with a Marxist-Leninist world view. This was a major issue. Minimising opportunities for corruption was another prominent concern.

I had to contend with the entrenched views of the old guard, and the pension provision was so abject that academics taught till they dropped. This old guard was *old*. My task was made possible by the support of a cadre of younger academics who had a better understanding of western ideas than their seniors and were anxious for reform. Eventually we'd constructed a modern syllabus from first-year undergraduate to final year PhD which not only made sense on paper but later seemed to work in practice. This whole modernising operation took in most of the former Soviet satellites and was financed by George Soros; enough to damn it in the eyes of the old guard. Towards the end of my stint I was asked by one senior academic how I would rate the Department. I mixed honesty with diplomacy and stressed the pressure of heavy teaching loads on research opportunities. "Ah yes", he mused, "research...do you know, even when one does find time to work in the library, the temperature isn't always conducive to the exploration of new ideas. I find it quite hard to motivate myself when the temperature outside is -40c, and it's not that much warmer inside. But it's not always like that. Sometimes it's +40c outside." The university itself was built by German prisoners of war at the end of the Second World War and I don't think it won many design awards. Sixty or so years later it was in a state of near collapse.

The hospitality of my young colleagues and the vibrancy of the city made my stays enjoyable but all visitors, me included, have to come to terms with one terrifying custom that might otherwise ruin them, hospitality. The locals always- *always* - give you for too much to eat and drink. On my first trip I got out of the airport finally at 4.15 am. A car from my small hotel had been sent to pick me up and the driver had been waiting for two hours. At the hotel, I told the young owner that I planned to sleep in and would come down for a light breakfast at 11 am. A *light* breakfast; I insisted, some yoghurt, a slice of toast, a piece of fruit and a cup of coffee. I explained that I had an important lunch appointment at 1 pm, at which I expected a substantial meal. He fully understood, So I came down to a breakfast comprising a large bowl of home-made yoghurt, a pack of six commercial yoghurts, two boiled eggs, two bananas , an apple and an orange, four slices of toast, four slices of rye bread, jam, marmalade, a range of local cheeses and a large pot of coffee. Thank goodness I'd stipulated a light breakfast.

I frequently found myself in a group of young post-graduates who were eager to practice their English but also to increase their knowledge of Britain and Europe. On one of my visits I was asked by an elegantly dressed young woman what chances England had in the soccer World Cup that year. Well, I replied, enunciating each word carefully, their prospects had been dealt a blow by an injury to one of their key forwards who had a poorly foot." Oh really", she replied with total assurance, "You surprise me. I understood from the World Service yesterday that Rooney's metatarsal problems had been rectified." There were many substantial potholes in the pavements and streets around: I could have done with one of the larger ones just then. Lovely people though some don't seem to have come to terms with this new-fangled idea of living life according to systems of law. Back now to Hull and the 1980s.

.

The Coming of Winter

Our small world of Concrete Towers was transformed after 1979 when the grocer's daughter from Lincolnshire raised an army of sharp-eyed, sharp-tongued, grey-suited reformers who transformed the way business was done in the Concrete Towers. These Grey Suits, the equivalent of Mao's Red Guards, were soon to be found everywhere around the Towers, as they were in the NHS, education, the police, the law. The Thatcherite state was maggoty with them. And they brought their own way of speaking. The philosophers Foucault and Marcuse talked about 'dominant discourse', a choice of vocabulary, syntax and idiom that set agendas. Marcuse called it 'Orwellian' whereas Orwell himself called it 'duck speak'. In setting the parameters of discussion, it deliberately wrong footed those who attempted to use normal everyday language. Take the little word 'So'. An innocuous little word commandeered by the Grey Suits for use at the beginning of most of their sentences to establish a relationship between speaker and listener; that of expert and layman. Beginning a sentence with a 'So' was a declaration of assumed dominance. "This is how it is. I *know*." Nowadays, unlike the Seventies, everyone begins their sentences with 'So'. It has been the only success of the Conservative policy to 'level up'.

But dominant discourse wasn't the heart of the problem. The Grey Suits had an agenda: they believed that the surest way to achieve optimal efficiency was target-based competition. They hollowed out just about every institution they touched, jettisoning civility, cooperation and tolerance. To borrow Ferdinand Tonnies phrase Thatcher turned universities from Gemeinschaften to Gesellschaften, from communities to companies. Through the 1980s the policies of her governments created havoc in higher education, as just about everywhere else, by enforcing massive cuts. As far as the university world was concerned the government operated at arm's length, via the University Grants Committee, which had been founded just after the First World War to oversee the funding of universities. It was given responsibility for trimming university budgets, though not of course in so many words.

In 1986.Universities were subjected to UGC 'visitations', a modern equivalent of the Spanish Inquisition. Funding for each institution was to be decided as a result of these visitations and there was a diminishing pot. Institutions went to great lengths to present themselves in the best possible light as intellectual and cultural beacons in their cities or regions. Hull's visitation began with a staggering own-goal. The Chairman had to come a day late and drove himself. On reaching the city he stopped to ask directions to the university only to be told several times, as I had been almost twenty years previously that Hull didn't have one. Some beacon. Many good people, fearful of the future of universities in these circumstances seemed to want to save them by chopping bits off. Sometimes big bits. There was no collective willingness to challenge the working premise of government policy. Institutions seemed determined to secure their own interests at the expense of others; just the kind of 'healthy' competition the Thatcherite strategy encouraged. Vice Chancellors and Principals attempted to swap departments like schoolboys swapping Panini stickers as the UGC applied the axe. : "I'll give you a Bobby Moore and a Jimmy Greaves for your Pat Crerand". "We'll give you our Italian Department, and throw in Classics for your American Studies, which'll gel with the research area of our top-notch English Department". Mystical phrases like "critical mass" struck fear into the breasts of many in smaller departments. Some 'experts' within the UGC calculated that a Physics Department, for example, needed 'x' numbers of staff to operate optimally, and Physics Departments with a number lower than 'x' would have to be considered for closure, or 'repurposing' through transfer to another department in their own institution or amalgamation with another Physics Department at a university 'nearish-by'.

We in Politics had a special interest in the potential wielding of this particular axe since some months earlier William Waldegrave, not the MP for Suffolk who died in 1554, though we might have preferred it to be him, but Thatcher's Parliamentary Under Secretary of State for Education, had visited Hull and on his departure dismissed the rumour doing the rounds that league tables of universities were being prepared as a basis for remodelling the system. Taking Hull as an example, he said, a university that might be thought of as Division Two - like the football team, he might have added - yet it contained at least two world-class Departments, Applied Physics and Politics. Less than a year later, Applied Physics was axed: it didn't have critical mass. We in Politics began to look nervously over our shoulders. What were house prices like in Sheffield?

The transformation from Gemeinschaferen to Gesellschaften required not only savage cuts in provision and services but paradoxically growth in what was to all intents and purposes new areas of management. Staff Development Offices mushroomed and behold: a whole new industry was created, populated, surprise, surprise by those ubiquitous young men and women in their grey suits. Later offices appeared dealing with the various forms of discrimination, each with a capacity for almost exponential growth. Who would doubt the wisdom of encouraging staff to develop their teaching skills, or of establishing procedures to combat discrimination? On the other hand, better teaching wasn't rewarded by promotion, so professional development would never attract serious staff attention; and a system of complaint procedures against all forms of injustice already existed. The assumption behind these developments seemed to be that the university's default position represented poor teaching, functional inefficiency, costliness and prejudice. Things didn't seem that way to us.

Of course, there were real inefficiencies in university administration - I've been writing about them - but these expensive new developments didn't seem to be the solution. In fairness to the government its increasing involvement in running universities represented the direct consequence of the growing importance and cost of higher education. Nowadays there are some 2.38 million students in higher education. When I was a student in the early Sixties there were just over 200,000. No wonder university inefficiencies went largely unnoticed. But the fact is that this growth had hardly begun before the Grey Suits arrived,

The Holy Grail of Cost Efficiency

The traditional administrative structure of most universities used to comprise Departments and Faculties. Suddenly it became obvious to everyone in a grey suit that this system was no longer fit for purpose. Departments and Faculties were to be swept away and replaced by a single tier: Schools. At Hull we'd had five Faculties and, if my memory serves, thirty-eight Departments. How much more cost-effective fourteen Schools and no Departments would be. Problem: how to decide which Departments went into which Schools. At Hull and in many other institutions the administration's masterstroke was to encourage the Departments themselves to decide. I cannot easily describe the turmoil that ensued, consuming a truly massive amount of time and energy and often causing corrosive friction. Politics eventually became part of the School of Social and Political Science, which made far better sense on paper than in reality. Finally, after a lot of blood had been mopped up, most Departments managed to construct new structures that 'worked' but I can think of none that welcomed the change or thought it brought many benefits. Inevitably there were some Departments that nobody wanted to get into bed with. Lumped together they formed what became widely known as The School of Residual Studies. But so many managerial lacunae were left when Faculties were abolished that a new university committee had hurriedly to be established to pick up the pieces.

As Chairman of the new 'pick-up-the-pieces' committee I was better placed than just about anyone to take the measure of the new structure. We made it work, just about, but after four years its overall ineffectiveness was acknowledged and the old Department/Faculty system was reinstated. A year or so after I left I was invited to act as External Examiner to another Yorkshire university. A Pro-Vice Chancellor took me to lunch and was delighted to tell me that *at last*, after a series of unpleasant confrontations, his institution had moved from Faculties to Schools. I would be delighted to hear, he went on, that their new structure was based on the Hull model. I asked if he was up-to-speed with the latest developments in the Hull model. "Why?" he asked, lips twitching nervously. "Well, they're just about to change back to Faculties; it seems to have been a failure." His jaw dropped, his podgy hands smacked down on the table, causing the eyebrows of some nearby fellow diners to rise. "Oh. Sweet Jesus.....*please* don't tell anybody here," he whispered.

And As if All This Weren't Enough...

One final area of change that I want to talk about: semesterisation. This is the process of transforming the traditional university calendar, comprising normally three terms each of ten weeks in to two semesters of up to fifteen weeks each. Most American and continental European institutions run on semesters. The British three-term structure was based upon the traditional law college terms. Christmas term began in October and ran for ten weeks until mid-December; spring from mid-January till the end of March and summer from mid-April till the end of June. From its founding in 1967 however the University of Stirling based its year on two semesters, winter and spring. Winter stretched from early September till just before Christmas and spring from mid-February till the end of June. It was the only British university to operate in this way.

Traditional courses would run for a whole academic year, at Stirling courses were semester-based. Having experienced both I saw their advantages and disadvantages. The three-term system seemed wasteful. Teaching didn't start properly until the second week of the first term and with no examination at the end of that term, some students would bunk off in the last week. The spring term formally provided ten full weeks of teaching, though again, with no examinations, there were often defections in the last week. In the summer term there were only three weeks of teaching followed by examinations. Officially course work for the following year would begin after the exams but obviously Final Year students would have left, and many returning students would have drifted off to find a summer job as soon as they had finished exams, so it seldom happened.

Standard semester systems such as Stirling's were much tighter. A fifteen-week winter semester allowed for eleven weeks teaching split in the middle by a 'reading week', a week for revision followed by two weeks of examinations. No possibility to bunk off in the last week, then! And this would be repeated in the spring semester, when the mid-semester reading week would coincide whenever possible with Easter.

I taught a course in Hull on Politics and Literature. It lasted what passed for a full year and comprised thirty-eight contact hours – two per week – and two 3,000word essays. Later I taught a similar course at Stirling. It comprised twenty-two contact hours – two per week – and one essay. In my judgement the Stirling system was more efficient and students and staff worked harder, though not massively harder. Game, set and match to the semester system then? Maybe. However, when you taught students under less pressure over the course of a whole academic year you got to know them, to see them develop, and to have more time and energy for personal interaction. It also meant that the students had greater freedom to pursue extra-curricular activities. That might mean boozing of course but it might also mean reading more widely, participating in clubs and societies, sports and so on, The biggest and most active student society at Hull when I was there, by some margin, provided a range of social services for the wider community, such as support for the elderly. Who can calculate the general educational value of diminished pressure and greater freedom?

From the government's perspective however, there was no contest: semesters offered a better use of limited resources. However the government left the details of semesterisation to individual universities. Most institutions, presumably because it involved fewer changes, continued to begin their year in October, thereby failing to complete a full semester by Christmas, so courses continued into January. Around the end of that month would come examinations, followed directly by the spring semester with new courses. But how could students properly choose their next semester's courses without knowing their results from the first semester? Moreover, that second semester would continue to be split by a four-week break at Easter. And this new framework offered no attraction to overseas students since it constituted no better match with their home university programmes. It represented a combination of clumsy governmental intervention followed by natural institutional inertia If this wasn't the worst of all worlds it must have come pretty close!

And in Conclusion

I spent quite a lot of my career in administration. For some this would constitute a stepping stone to a Faculty Deanship or Pro-Vice Chancellorship, or who knows what? This was the path I decided to avoid. True, I ran a department for fifteen years but in my experience the real work is done by the departmental secretary. I was lucky enough over the years to work with three women of charm, dedication and administrative ability. They made me look quite competent without my having to try too hard.

Being involved in decisions that shaped one's institution even at this level can have a narcotic effect which is enhanced if one believes oneself to be good at it. On that point I was ambivalent. Generally speaking when I spent most of my time running things I used to think that I was much better at research. On the other hand when I was researching and writing I used to be convinced I was much better at administration. There are those, mostly scientists, who marry administration and research successfully; they manage large project-based research teams some of whose work directly benefits society at large. I found no equivalent in my own area of research. Finally although administering was far more lucrative, believing as I did that universities were heading in the wrong direction was a major disincentive to helping them get there, even if you finished up richer.

There was something fundamentally dysfunctional about the nature of the role of the Concrete Towers in society, a problem that Thatcher's policies didn't address let alone solve. The Concrete Tower does not, *cannot* perform the function of the traditional Ivory Tower. It no longer has the primary task of educating the elite. In fact what many university degrees nowadays provide isn't education in the broader, cultural sense but training. Now that is not such a bad thing if that training were to produce suitably qualified graduates in areas where society needs them: a kind of supply-and-demand relationship. There is indeed a supply and demand relationship, but the demand which universities supply comes from student preferences, not society's needs, and these are decidedly not two sides of the same coin. In my career at different times there have been surges in demand - fashions – for a variety of disciplines and universities responded by enhancing their provision in these areas, some even creating provision almost on the hoof. Whether society has a need for these particular skills or whether the academic quality of the provision created to meet changing fashions is fit for purpose seems to have been of secondary importance.

I alluded earlier to the number of British lap dancers with a university degree; it might easily be in Law, because we educate *far* more lawyers than even our litigious society needs. It's often argued that a Law degree is a sound intellectual base for most future careers, though perhaps not lap-dancing, but the great majority who come to read Law want a career in the Law. This is not the best way or organising higher education.

All things considered, administration in the Concrete Tower wasn't for me. I suppose what I'd always really aspired to was to become an old-fashioned scholar and towards the end of my career, at Stirling, that's more or less what I became.

7. *In Corpore Sano*

When I was a youth in the Fifties on the Isle of Dogs, universities meant only one thing: the annual boat race. In those days not many families had a TV and even for those who did there was little mainstream sport for them to watch on their small, flickering, black-and-white screens. *The* boat race – Oxford v Cambridge - was a major sporting event in the national calendar, much more so than it is today, even for those of us who only got to see it later on *Pathé News* at the local cinema. When Winston Smith, in Orwell's *1984*, interrogates an ancient prole about life in the 'good old days', pre-revolution, it's the Boat Race he remembers. "Terribly rowdy they used to get on Boat Race night", he says. Back in the 1880s the great William Morris had a house near the Thames and would throw parties on Boat Race Day, which his wife detested because they became so rowdy. The race was always held on a Saturday in spring and on that day, as on every other Saturday, I would go to Saturday Morning Pictures at the Odeon Greenwich. The weekly cartoons and serials like Flash Gordon and Roy Rogers were always spliced together by a communal sing-along led by a larger-than-life, flashily dressed compere. On Boat Race Day he would begin by asking which of us was for Cambridge and which for Oxford. Everyone would have a favourite and almost magically we were always divided pretty evenly. The competition as to whether Oxford could out-sing Cambridge or vice versa was keen. So universities had this specifically sporting connotation for us.

The Corinthian Spirit

Growing into adolescence, I became aware of universities in a broader sporting context; the idea of the gentlemen scholars, who had the time to devote themselves to sport, officially as amateurs, was part of the national culture. When later I represented the school at soccer I was made well aware of the importance of the Corinthian legacy when the spirit of C.B. Fry – and I don't mean his later notorious pro-fascistic tendencies - still lived. One of the principal games of each cricket season in those days was 'Gentlemen' versus 'Players', amateurs versus professionals. The fixture had begun before the Napoleonic Wars and was last played at Scarborough in 1962 after which the distinction between the two was dropped. Even the hard-nosed Yorkshire team, almost all of whom had been professionals for decades, was traditionally captained by a 'gentleman', an amateur. Most of these amateurs were university types, so the relationship between universities and sport captured in that word 'Corinthian' was well understood and widely, if not universally practiced. Scholarship and sport were joined at the hip. If you were going up to university you would expect to play a lot of sport. *Mens sana in corpore sano.*

As an undergraduate I certainly gave a lot of time to sport, especially soccer and then, after a transfer of allegiance, to rugby. I spent many an afternoon in the gym: too many in fact. When I was a postgraduate at the Victoria University of Wellington and seeking some recreational activity to prevent the body from collapsing, joining the rugby club seemed a no-brainer. I soon became acutely aware that rugby in New Zealand is *not* a recreation; it is a religious devotion. Even 3rd XV players like me received a tailor made, personalised fitness programme: mine was for loose forwards. It didn't help my self-esteem that the entire nation, including the women, knew more about the game than I and most of them were better at playing it, but I soldiered on notwithstanding, following my programme, for two seasons. In my last game I smashed my collar bone and decided pretty soon after that, when we returned to Blighty, I would take up something slightly more genteel.

If I'm to be accurate *I* didn't break my collar bone; it was broken for me by a large gentleman of the Polynesian variety whose ferocious tackle took me to the bottom of a ruck. Not only was that the last match of the season, it was in the last phase of play in the last match of my second and last season. As we left the field I was aware of a dull pain which got worse as I showered and changed. I found if I cradled that elbow, my right, in the palm of my left hand and took some pain killers, it was bearable. And although the pain eased after a couple of days with the help of those tablets, I continued to adopt this pose for the next several months, totally unaware of the fact that my collar bone had been shattered. I now know that what I did to manage the pain was pretty much what a doctor would have prescribed anyway.

Back in Yorkshire the following autumn I confirmed my decision not to continue chasing oval balls. I knew there was a lot I'd miss but I didn't much fancy the idea of spending my weekends away from home being pummelled by some overweight, evil forty year old embittered bank clerk in the cloying mud of a smoky West Riding town. I wondered which of the non-contact indoor sports most closely resembles rugby? Answer: squash... at least, the way I played it.

There are two particular sports, cricket and rowing, which I regret never having tried, the former only because I love it. La Rochefoucauld said that not being a religious people, the English had invented cricket to give them some idea of eternity. I wonder if he could have been persuaded to swap eternity for Heaven. I never played it, not even at school where I played tennis in the summer, but have always enjoyed watching it probably above all sports. There's so much more to it. As for rowing I inherited the gene from my father, who worked on the river. I had a whitewater rafting experience on the Urubamba River in Peru some years ago. We were given instructions on what to do with the paddles by our Peruvian skipper and then we promptly set out into the rapids to dice with death. At one point he said to me: "You *ver'* good my frien'– you done dees before!" Not true, and I'm not even a quick learner. I just think it was, as the Shetlanders say, i' da blud: I was a natural. As for the sports I did play, I can't claim any degree of skill, being inhibited by the damage incurred by a motor bike accident as well as being depleted in the collarbone department.

All the same, my enjoyment wasn't limited by this lack of prowess. Some of the most memorable moments of my university career were spent in the pursuit, often fruitless, of that little black ball fizzing around a usually cold squash court. Squash dominated my leisure life at Hull for about a quarter of a century.

Breaking Down Barriers

Amongst the welcoming material I got as a new member of staff at Hull was an invitation to squash. Squash was by far the most popular sport amongst members of staff at Hull, another good reason for writing about it. It seemed to have a strong appeal for academics, especially of course the younger ones, though it was played by some in their sixties. You could spot these a mile off by their wooden rackets, voluminous shorts and spindly legs. Would-be squashers were invited to peruse the ladder on the club notice board in the sports centre and select an opponent at what you considered to be an appropriate level in the pecking order, phone them and arrange a game. Two of the more notable features of my game were a certain tactical naivety and lack of subtlety; I hit the ball hard, ran fast and looked menacing, a style that probably owed quite a lot to rugby. I thought I could legitimately aim at a name just about half way up the ladder and selected my victim at random, one George Crosby.

As things turned out, I was a bit too much for George and rather overwhelmed him. We were watched briefly from the balcony by an ex-Indian Army officer, Arthur Horsefield, who worked in the Estates Office, and who captained the University Staff 'C' team in which George featured. In the changing rooms afterwards George introduced us. He explained to Arthur that I'd outplayed him and could probably manage a berth in the second team. Arthur favoured me with a dismissive glance and then, promptly ignoring me, told George in no uncertain terms that it didn't do for one to go round encouraging just anybody to join the club especially, though he didn't say this, if they might beat one. As to representing the university one needed to exhibit a proper sportsmanlike – Corinthian – quality the like of which he'd seen no evidence in my game. George stood his ground however and gave me the number of the captain of the second team. I subsequently phoned the number and Peter Andrews said he'd already heard from George and would like me to appear as No. 4 in the B team the following Tuesday. I was chuffed. We hadn't met, Peter and I, so when I turned up a bit early on Tuesday and introduced myself to the guy umpiring a game, I assumed he would be Peter. No, Peter was playing. One player was skilful, playing the angles and lobbying intelligently, the other rushed about, claiming lets (I'll explain shortly) every time he was caught out of position. Well, according to Arthur's formula, Peter *had* to be the skilful one, not the bully, who nevertheless contrived to win. No, it transpired that Peter was the winner.

For those unfamiliar with squash, a little explanation is in order. I said earlier that squash reminded me a little of rugby. This is because it encourages players to compete for the space at the centre of the court in order to dominate rallies by playing the ball where your opponent isn't. To play the ball he has to come round you. Players in the higher leagues will nearly always contrive to give their opponents a reasonable view of the ball. If they don't, their opponent can legitimately complain that he's being baulked and ask for a let. If the umpire agrees, the point is replayed. At our level the more devious players, if caught out of position, would crash into their opponent in the centre of court and claim a let. And there was no limit to the number of lets you could claim. From time to time, you would meet an opponent who inadvertently just got in your way. More rarely you would play an opponent who advertently got in your way and claimed lets whenever they got out of position. Physical clashes, some of them accidental, were not uncommon, Good adjudication was vitally important; in squash as in rugby.

I played at No.4 for the rest of the season for the B team, with Peter as No.3. I won most of my games and he lost most of his: it was clear to me that he was past his best and slowing down. One Friday afternoon at the end of that season he challenged me to a friendly to decide who should play at 3 the following season, I quickly beat him 3-0. He insisted on another game which I won 3-0. Come on, he said, I'd been lucky: surely I'd to allow him another game? I beat him 3-0. I never saw Peter play another game; he turned to golf. My squash had improved, as his had deteriorated, but with me it was still very much 'light blue touch paper and stand well back'. I would have to seek some serious coaching.

Another Dimension

The university boasted two squash coaches, Ian and Wynn. Ian was past his peak, probably early fifties, but supremely fit with a well-balanced all-round game. He tried to dominate the court by sheer physical presence and speed of movement. Wynn was slighter, trimmer, a player of subtle lobs and angles. I considered myself lucky to be given Wynn as my coach. He always wore a pair of baggy shorts, a shapeless Fred Perry shirt and an ancient pair of plimsolls. In short he was about as unlike Ian as you could imagine. Wynn began to improve my overall strategic sense, got me moving around the court more, and widened my range of shots, which wasn't too difficult. I felt I improved that term and was dismayed when Wynn told me he would be leaving before the start of the next term to take up a position in Melbourne. If only he could have resisted the charms of Victoria I might have become a half-decent squash player.

I'd never much liked Ian, who took me on after Wynn's departure, even less so when I discovered in our first session that his *modus operandi* was to finish each coaching session by playing a set against his charge. I don't know if the scoring system has changed, but back then you scored points only on your own service and to win a set you had to score 9 points, or if the score got to 8-8 you had to get two clear points in the lead. What Ian did was to allow his charge to get to, say 7-1 and then smash them off the court dismissively winning the set 9-7. What kind of senior player gets his kicks by ritually humiliating learners? I didn't like his expensive cream shorts, or his stylish matching shirt with blue piping, or his state-of-the art trainers. Nor the fact that he sped effortlessly around you as if jet propelled. You'd catch him, or so you thought, in the backhand corner and then play a killing dink to the forehand front of the court. Ian would be through you like a dose of salts, leaving nothing in his wake but a whiff of expensive aftershave. Now at the front of the court he would play a deadly cross-court boast that left you floundering. When he wanted to, Ian could annihilate any learner and he always seemed to want to, but first, to make it satisfying, he had to make you think you'd finally got him this time.

One Friday morning he let me get to 7 before firing up the boosters. I'm thinking, I've only got to force *one* error from him, take serve, and I could win this game. So I went for it. But steadily he devoured my lead till it got to 7-7 when I regained serve, which hadn't been part of his plan. I fortuitously won the next point to lead 8-7. Only one bit of luck to win! Ian won service back only for me to bounce back immediately with a jammy miss-hit return that wrong-footed him. I'm serving for the set again- and this time as the rally developed I played a cross-court dink that Wynn himself would have been proud of. Ian was up and across like a whippet and somehow got to my shot, but managed only to lob a gentle return more or less straight to me and at the most inviting of heights. He was at my mercy. A number of thoughts flashed through my mind. I knew I could win the point and the set and that I would be doing it for every mouse with whom Ian had toyed over the years. There he was, off-balance and out of position at the front of the court. As I said, at my mercy

If I'd been in Ian's position, what would I have done? I would have pushed as hard as I could off the sidewall and into centre of the court, just hoping that I might intercept the inevitable pass or lob. Little chance of success, but you can't just roll over can you? Yes, that's what I'd have done. And what would my best response to this move be, assuming Ian attempts the same? To hammer the ball as near as possible to the place that Ian had just vacated, so that the ball crashes around his legs and flies past him. Game over.

No experienced player in the civilised world would have done what I'd scripted Ian to do. In such circumstances they would forfeit the point, sit back on their haunches and raise their hand in acknowledgement. The opponent, in this case me would just have caught the ball and claimed the point. This is exactly what Ian was expecting, so he sat on his haunches, hand raised aloft and surrendered.

What *actually* happened though was that just at the moment of surrender I had unleashed the Hammer of Thor, aimed at the spot he was supposed to vacate. Hard to calculate even roughly the speed at which the ball encountered Ian's gluteus maximus: probably something approaching Mach 2. Imagine my horror at this turn of events and then reflect, as I have often, on how pale and insignificant my horror would have been compared to Ian's. Of course I tried to apologise but Ian, imagining that what I had done to have been deliberate, pushed past me with a look like thunder. What must Arthur have said to George Crosbie when he heard? With no word exchanged on court or after, my name was removed from the coaching list and Ian and I never spoke again. But I didn't lose my place in the team.

All in the Mind

Squash became a central feature of my life at Hull, not just because I played it to a serious level, but because it provided quick release from academic concerns. In my experience the word university is a misnomer: it conjures up an institution bringing together a range of academic disciplines under an inclusive cultural umbrella. In truth, most members of a department have little or nothing to do with colleagues from other departments apart from those sharing Combined or Joint Honours degree programmes. Playing representatively meant you'd to get a couple of friendlies in each week, to keep fit and to keep your eye in and so I got to know a range of opponents from every part of the university. Only one other member of my own Department played squash seriously. He sometimes featured for the B team but didn't want the responsibility of playing regularly. We had a similar style and were both on the large side for squash. I was fourteen and a half stone; he couldn't have been much less, and we both tried to hit the ball hard. We played each other regularly over the years, though not ever so often. Overall I would say I won about 60% of our games. One encounter sticks in the mind above all the rest.

We had a game arranged for one Monday at the start of the Easter vacation. As it happened there had been a programme on the TV that Sunday evening called, if I remember correctly, *The Mind Game*. It was an analysis of the importance of mental states when playing sport. Its main thesis was that, rather than allowing the brain to solve problems during play, consciousness actually got in the way of our instinctive abilities; the best thing a sportsperson could do was take consciousness out of the equation. Amongst the contributors was an American tennis coach whose methods aimed to achieve just this mental state. He would teach trainees six basic tennis shots, three forehands, three backhands, and get them to work on these until they came naturally. He would then play against them and insist that during rallies, when going to make a shot, they shout 'bounce!' loudly before striking the ball. Why? Well, he believed that having mastered the basics, they would *instinctively* produce the most appropriate shot. What the player had to do was to focus on remembering to shout "bounce", allowing nature to take its course in respect of the tennis ball. Eventually you would graduate to mouthing 'bounce' silently, but the point was that in concentrating on saying it at all, you couldn't be thinking about your shot. But your body could. He swore by this method.

It had to be worth a shout, don't you think, especially in what promised to be a hard-fought battle? I launched my new plan that Monday. As the match began I was much more composed than usual and, as I silently mouthed 'bounce', I seemed to have all the time in the world and put just the right amount of weight into each of my increasingly confident shots. Well, to be more accurate, 'I' didn't: my instinct did. And I, or 'it', annihilated my opponent. He got increasingly red in the face but said not a word throughout and as we returned to an empty changing room, looking black as thunder, he hurled his racket at the wall and broke into a tirade of blistering expletives. As we were drying off after the shower, and after he'd calmed down, I ventured to ask had he watched TV the previous evening? He had. Had he seen a programme called *The Mind Game*? He erupted: "Yeh, and what a shed load a' *shit*", he thundered. "Fuckin' *rubbish*." The image of two rather large, rather sweaty middle-aged gentlemen crashing around a squash court silently mouthing 'bounce!', the one feeling he'd found the key to squash success , the other beside himself with humiliation, would have been something for the cognoscenti of mind games to cherish. And I hadn't the heart to tell him.... Unfortunately the transformation wasn't life changing after all; it seemed to make no difference subsequently.

Around tea time that day I got an irate phone call from his wife who wanted to know what I'd been doing with her husband who had spent the entire afternoon on his back in the front room with his legs up against the wall, suffering from piles. Injury to insult.

A Team Sport

The university sponsored four squash teams, A, B, C, D, and as I've said I played for the B team. In the A team were some gifted sportsmen, as indeed there were in B, but maybe just a bit older or less dedicated. One such was Roger, who played for the B team for about as long as I did. Initially he played at No.1, but after some years moved down to accommodate Gavin, a ferociously fit former hockey player of note. Gavin wouldn't have claimed to be a gifted squash player but with his supreme fitness would grind opponents into the ground. Remorselessness is a virtue, or at least an attribute, not to be underestimated. The world squash champion of those days was Jonah Barrington who freely admitted, indeed boasted of the fact that any number of his opponents were better players than he. But at the end of most of his encounters he would be the last man standing. Like Gavin, he squashed his opponents...slowly but surely.

So Roger settled in mainly at No.2. We must have played each other hundreds of times over the years and he would certainly have won more often than I. All the same, if I needed to, I could always beat Roger: I knew his secret. Roger hated cheats, and squash, as I've shown, has plenty of scope for cheats because of the problem of lets. Now if he found himself playing such an opponent, as soon as he became sure that the man was cheating intentionally, Roger would simply give up, and just go through the motions, get off court as quickly as possible. He would be unable to force himself to compete. So if you were playing Roger and your life was depending on it, just claim a few dodgy lets and victory would be assured.

At No.4 was Geoff, for whom the phrase 'small but perfectly formed' was originally coined. Though Geoff was short, stocky and bald and from a distance looked like a large broad bean, you underestimated him at your peril, and many of his opponents did just that. Wily wasn't the word for Geoff. Others played regularly for the B team over the years and there were fringe players who came and went, and they emerged from all parts of the university. A softly spoken and personable Welsh physicist called John played for several years and he also would often turn out at No.1. His considerable skill wasn't matched by comparable aggression though and he was sometimes beaten by lesser opponents...such as me, now and again. Barry from the Estates Office fortunately lasted less than one season. I think he might have been an android; many in Estates were. Quite devoid of all social graces, this monosyllabic Lancastrian used to train by running round the sports field for general fitness, as indeed most of us did, but uniquely Barry always carried his squash racket with him and would go through his range of shots as he ran. I asked him about this: he said he wanted to make his racket feel like a part of his body. When he played Barry would unintentionally get in his opponent's way all the time. Nobody liked playing him: and that was his main weapon.

The Club president was an Old Etonian patrician whose squash gear owed a great deal to the 1920s style and it suited him. He took me to one side once and asked if I would explain to him what mortgages were and how they worked: he was minded to buy a second home in a North Riding village. He was in his fifties in those days and played only friendlies but he doubled as President of the Hull and East Riding League, a post he held for twenty or so years. He exhibited a formidably comprehensive memory of fixtures and results in all the local divisions since the reign of William of Orange and could spout these endlessly, in detail when asked, and frequently when not asked. He was roundly dismissive of my squash playing; I rather got the impression that he was of the Arthur Horsefield persuasion and thought that the image of the game would be improved if the oiks could be kept away. Towards the end of my squash career the university had to disband the A team when three of its stalwarts moved elsewhere. Rather than promote the B team as the *de facto* A team the president dispensed with the title 'A Team' altogether. He thought the title should be put in storage until players worthy of the classification emerged. Sometimes one's best just isn't good enough. Appropriately he taught Classics.

All the same, we 'B teamers' got about, with matches not only around the environs of Hull but as far afield as Scarborough to the north, Bridlington to the east and Pocklington to the west. Once, but only once, we even ventured into *terra incognita*, south over the Humber and played a match in Brigg. Being a winter sport meant some hairy journeys; Garrowby Hill in the January fogs isn't necessarily as attractive as David Hockney would have you believe. Not surprising many of the venues were similar, local civic sports arenas mostly, but some were highly idiosyncratic. The courts at Reckitt and Colman abutted the laundries and so even in mid-winter enjoyed a South Asian climate, and rallies would go on forever, with the ball refusing to die. British Aerospace, on the other hand, played on an isolated court in the middle of a vast concrete concourse at Brough. The ball was like a lump of black pudding from beginning to end and long rallies were almost unheard of. But wherever we played and however well or badly we did, we'd have grand evenings, with each game leading to an hour or two in a local bar socialising with the opposition.

The most memorable evening followed a game against the masters of Pocklington School. They took us to an old coaching inn up in the Wolds. Though we drank only moderately we weren't restricted to a pint each in these days. When I went up to the bar half an hour before last orders at 10.30, I noticed that the menu board still stood on the bar, so I asked were they still serving sandwiches. Anything on the board, was the reply. "Sausage and chips?" I ventured incredulously. *Anything* was the reply. Now apart from us eight squashers the only people in the bar were a middle-aged couple who looked like locals sitting discreetly in a quiet corner and I noted that they had just ordered fresh drinks, so the 10.30 closing wasn't likely to be an issue. After consultation with my colleagues I returned with an order for eight sausage-and-chips. It was superb and amazingly there was still time afterwards for a last round at 11.30. About ten minutes later that couple took their leave of the landlady and she came over to us. "Sup up lads, copper's left".

Not all Sweat and Grunt... But Mostly Sweat and Grunt

Though post-match socialising was probably the most important part of the proceedings, don't think for a moment that we didn't take our on-court responsibilities seriously. Nobody gave up without a real struggle and people would turn out to play even when full of cold or generally unwell. I've mentioned the chivalrous Roger who played at No.2, one position above me. His wife told me that her man had got off his sick-bed more than once to come and play. His games against one particular opponent acquired the status of legend over the years. The opponent in question played for British Aerospace, an engineer with the improbable name of Alf Rivet. These games were always nip and tuck, always five-setters with long rallies. They always drove each other to the limit. I was umpiring their match on one cold November evening, on the University's old court, a purpose built structure standing on its own and so particularly susceptible to the cold. After two sets, each man. having won one, Roger asked to leave the court. When he didn't soon return I went to find him. He was in the toilets heaving up. Back he came to take the third set but lose the fourth. At this point Alf left the court and walked out of the building to throw up in the field. The fifth and final set was a cliff-hanger but Roger eventually won that one. Fortunately this had been the first game of an increasingly cold evening and the others were over much more quickly so that we could escape to the warmth of the bar well before closing. This life-and-death rivalry between Roger and Alf must have lasted five or six years with Fortuna bestowing her gifts more or less equally.

My own most memorable battle by a long way was against Hull YPI and I found myself playing the last match, after three pretty short matches. We were 1-2 down and needed the draw to secure our survival in that division. All down to me then. I was up against a tall, bearded, hard-hitting opponent who seemed to be just a little too good for me in every area of the game. He took the first two sets comfortably 9-1, 9-1, and was leading 8-1 in the third: one point away from the most comprehensive of victories. Except at that point I won serve and slowly began to match him shot for shot and fight my way into that third set, which I eventually won. Two sets to one. He was annoyed but unruffled. The fourth set went the way of the others. I was 8-1 down and he was one point away from victory...again. And I won serve and started the fight back. The rallies went on. I began to match him and even wear him down and won that fourth set too. By this time I was getting massive encouragement from my comrades, the name Lazarus rebounding from the walls, if more in hope than expectation. Two sets all now, and on to the fifth and final set.

Once more he went off like a rocket and got to 8-1...again. One point more for victory... again. At that point I broke his serve... again. I now began to outmanoeuvre him and as the rallies stretched out. I could sense that he was tiring. Slowly I started to claw my way into the final set point by hard-fought point until we reached 8-8 and he let out the most fearful howl. I knew he was broken and that if I just kept playing steadily, nothing flash, he would make a mistake. Miraculously I won the game. Strange to relate but my euphoria didn't appear to be shared by my colleagues in the gallery: no anticipated salutations to Lazarus. Only polite applause. I went up to retrieve my sweater and to receive some sort of accolades from friend and foe. No a bit of it. A few perfunctory congratulations, followed, by general contumely: apparently the match had gone on past closing time and we wouldn't be getting the customary drink. If I remember right, a party had been thrown for Lazarus.

The Fair Sex

Only in the last two years or thereabouts of the more than twenty I played for the Staff did the social side of the game begin to lose out to the actual squash. This was largely because teenage males and younger women came more into the game, and they tended to be either too serious to socialise or too young to go drinking. Earlier it had been rare to find oneself up against a female opponent and the physicality of the game, at our modest level anyway, usually gave a man the advantage. I recall only one game against a female opponent in the early years, a large jolly lady of indeterminate age called Bunty who used words like "corker" when congratulating opponents on their shots, rather than chasing after them. Some years later however I turned up at one home fixture to find that I had another female opponent. She was standing next to the umpire, smoking. She was in her forties, I would have guessed, so about ten years older than I and, to be honest, looked a bit heavier. I didn't expect many problems.

Sure enough by hitting the ball low and hard and moving her around the court I raced to a two-set lead. I'd hardly broken sweat. Victory was assured, so I decided that instead of knocking her off the court I would change tactics, slow down and indulge in a game of delicate chips and lobs that I had been working on. I felt confident that I would beat her whatever game I played. I hit one arching, high backhand lob that was due to die in the back corner. Except as it passed over her head she rose high, arched her back and met it sweet as a nut, dinking a delicate shot across-court that hit just above the tin and died. An amazing piece of unrepeatable good fortune. I lobbed again, and again, and yet again – and each time her incredible good fortune *was* repeated. And she started to win points. She took that third set. This was just the kind of workout I needed, and in the fourth set I continued to play with great subtlety; so she won that set too. Two all!

At this point I decided to revert to my accustomed smash-and-bash. By now though she had her eye well and truly in and matched me shot for shot. She began to hit the ball nearly as hard as I and with considerably greater accuracy. She went on to a crushingly comprehensive victory. She went off home so I didn't get the chance to buy her a drink, but I did have an interesting chat with her team mates over a beer. I couldn't understand it, I complained: losing after being so much on top. "Aye", said one, "We were a bit puzzled too. What was the thinking behind changing to a lobbing game against a former English badminton international?"

Rubbing Shoulders with Power

I met some fascinating opponents over the years. One in particular stands out even now, more than thirty years later. We were playing an annual fixture against RAF Leconfield and my opponent was new to the base. He told an amazing story. He had gone to Oxford on an RAF scholarship to take a Dual Honours degree in French and Italian and had finished with a First. His achievement was acknowledged before long with a posting to NATO headquarters in Brussels as the aide-de-camp to a senior RAF officer, with whom he didn't get on from the beginning. Matters came to a head when he was given a bollocking by this immediate boss in front of his fellow officers for speaking to his opposite numbers from France and Italy in French and Italian. But, my new friend pointed out, the RAF had just paid for a three-year degree course precisely so that he might be able to converse with them in their own language. His boss explained in the strongest terms that these bastards should be speaking English like everyone else, and if he wanted to stay at HQ, my friend should act accordingly.

It happened soon after that an invitation came for his boss to attend a lunch-time gathering of top brass the following Sunday: dress informal. The message was duly passed on bosswards but mysteriously 'informal' became trimmed down to 'formal'. When that gathering took place the British presence rather stood out; like the pretentious tosser some of his European colleagues thought he was. And wasn't the boss pleased! Our young squasher found himself reassigned forthwith back to domestic duties in the UK, which required him to travel to RAF stations all around the land, preparing for a visit to be conducted three months later by some invariably minor member of the Royal Family. Hence his appearance in the East Riding. He would be in charge of co-ordinating all preparations. Visit over he would be moved on to the next lucky station. Not surprisingly our man told us that a career change was imminent.

My contacts with parliamentarians led to a memorable encounter between the B team of the University of Hull Staff Squash Club and the Parliamentary Squash Club. In one of my interviews with MPs the subject of squash had arisen and this backbencher had offered us a challenge. We arranged to play on a Friday morning several months later and sure enough, one pleasant day in early May we took an early morning train from Hull Paragon with a prestigious match, a pub lunch, an afternoon visit to the National Gallery, an Italian meal and a well-reviewed play in the evening planned. It turned out to be as good a day as it sounded. Of the parliamentarians we faced, one was a local MP, one a member of the House of Lords, one a Junior Minister and Mrs Thatcher's blue-eyed boy, and the fourth was my opponent Jocelyn Cadbury. Apart from being a skilful squash player he was delightful company. We were stunned to hear of his suicide a few months later. John Moore, the Junior Minister, had come to the fixture straight from the airport in a ministerial car, having asked his driver to buy him a complete squash kit, since he hadn't the time to go home and get his own. I've no reason to believe that this constituted an illegal charge on the public purse, even though he was a Tory. The local MP might like to have have been described as 'colourful'. A staunch Thatcherite, fierce enemy of the European Union, John Townend earned notoriety later by referring to the British as a 'mongrel race' — and he wasn't talking about the mixture of Saxons, Vikings and Celts. He tried to milk information from us about alleged managerial problems at Hull University. We didn't much care for him. We drew the game, had a memorable day and got home mellow, and late.

Overall, would I say that my efforts to acquiring a 'corpore sano' helped towards a 'mens sana', or did it divert my attention from more important career matters? I don't think I ever had much choice: I *needed* sport and squash was an important part of my life at Hull. I got more than twenty years of pleasure from playing squash in however mediocre a fashion, and am still in regular contact with several fellow squashers. And it certainly helped to keep me relatively fit and healthy. As a bonus I got to know quite a lot about how my university looked from many perspectives. But one of the best memories of my squash playing days, which always brings a warm glow, is my victory at Hull YPI, the curmudgeonly reception from my team mates notwithstanding. Nice one Lazarus, I think to myself, you did it!

8. *Over My Shoulder*

After forty-four years of teaching in the Concrete Towers I finally hung up my biro. Or almost. Two or three years after retiring from Stirling I was asked to teach some courses at the University of Edinburgh's Institute for Lifelong Learning. One was an intensive three-day course on Orwell and it attracted some interesting students, none local, including a teacher of English from Japan who, seeing my course advertised, felt motivated to fulfil a long-term promise he'd made himself, and come on a three-week trip, anchoring a week of it in Scotland around my course. A longer course on Politics and Literature the following year attracted a mixture, from two full-time undergraduates to an elegant eighty-four year old who immediately told me she wasn't going to do any of the recommended reading but would discuss the topics each week with her daughter. Every Wednesday our dowager came better primed than anyone. I enjoyed being part of that contribution to the intellectual life of the city. It paid peanuts, but then, that's what we monkeys love. Unfortunately even the little money they had ran out and my services were dispensed with and so I retired for good.

If three or four years at university are supposed to be transformative, what d'you get from forty-four years, and how does what one gets relate to what one gives? The key to understand what the Concrete Towers are supposed to be about is to grasp the crucial relationship between research and teaching, a relationship that is, or should be, at the heart of the Concrete Towers experience. What I shall try to do in this final chapter is show what I got out of my research and how it shaped me and hence my teaching.

Rubbing Shoulders with my Betters

I began my career interviewing and writing about Liberals, amongst whom Jo Grimond, then party leader, stood out. He was the first senior politician I interviewed and one of the most impressive. Jeremy Thorpe, his successor, had an inspirational manner and seemed enormously capable, but would you want to buy a used car from him? After the Norman Scott case he inspired a memorable piece of graffiti: *Vote Liberal or we'll shoot your dog!* Paddy Ashdown was another charismatic Liberal, or rather Liberal Democrat and seemed a genuinely decent bloke. If I had to choose one to spend an evening with it would be Charlie Kennedy who seemed to have everything needed to become a major political leader including a lot of charm. His political demise and subsequent death were tragic. The politician who made the greatest impression on me as a leader, though, wasn't a Liberal but Labour's John Smith. His death was such a loss to the political life of this country. Meeting these figures and many more backbenchers added another dimension to my research and, to be candid, intermittently lit up my life. I would have to exclude Sir Edward Heath from this generalisation.

Mislaid Idealism

I started my political studies in 1959 when Harold Macmillan was Prime Minister. When I went up to Sheffield I would have confidently claimed to be a solid Labour supporter, but then I discovered John Stuart Mill's essay *On Liberty* which had a profound effect on my unformed young mind. I became what was known at the time as a Lib-Lab, believing in community, participation and equality.

New Zealand in 1964, I discovered, when I went to research for my PhD, was just about as equal a society as one could wish for: no real poverty or ostentatious wealth. Almost uniquely the average income was close to the typical income. There were no slums and no disaffected urban working class, and if there was any racial disharmony it wasn't immediately apparent. The Prime Minister's number was listed in the public telephone directory. New Zealand's social values had largely been shaped by those early years of colonisation when survival depended on the capacity of settlers to work together in communities, a self-help society which could hardly have succeeded without the full participation of the great majority of settlers. Notions of community and participation were as important in contemporary Kiwi society as was equality. Paradise, then, for us Lib-Labs.

Except, as you've guessed, it wasn't. It was an honest, caring society in which, in my experience, nobody needed to lock their door at night. It was also *profoundly* conformist. Imagine Huxley's *Brave New World,* except that everybody's a Beta. Like William Morris, your average Kiwi, and remember they were mostly average, believed that no man was good enough to be another man's master. The idea of waiting at table and the kind of relationship between diner and waiter that this normally involved was anathema at least to the males of the species. In Wellington at the time there was only one 'posh' restaurant and it got away with it largely by virtue of being French. Trying to be different was frowned upon because it was seen as trying to appear better. We're all Betas, get used to it!

I went to buy a pair of jeans once and could find literally only one style. A pair of jeans is a pair of bloody jeans, right? Impossible to deny that such a society has a lot to commend it, but in my experience the level of conformity was numbing. On our ship going out to NZ were dozens of teachers who travelled out for free, though if they returned to the UK within three years they would have to refund their fare. As we approached New Zealand each received a package informing them where they were being sent to teach and offering stern general guidance on demeanour and behaviour. This included the advice that if they wore a beard they should seriously consider shaving it off before arrival because New Zealanders didn't like beards.

An American academic working in Wellington wrote a critique of New Zealand society in 1960 called *The Fern and the Tiki.* Though it appeared in the index of each of the three or four libraries I went to, it was not on the shelves, nor could any of the librarians locate it when I asked. When I spoke to my supervisor about this he offered to lend me his copy - wrapped in brown paper! Mick Jagger is reputed to have claimed that on the first Stones visit in the Sixties, as the plane descended into Wellington, the steward asked passengers to please put their seats in the upright position, fasten their seat belts and set their watches to local time by putting them back 50 years.

My belief in equality became, to say the least, more nuanced. When we'd been in the country for a year or so an academic colleague in Sociology told me that he'd planned to take his family out sailing the previous Sunday, but when he'd got up early to make breakfast he'd discovered the kitchen floor several inches deep in water. So he'd phoned his plumber, explaining the urgency of his predicament. The plumber was sympathetic but explained that he was unable to help that day since he was taking the family sailing. We're all Betas, mate.

I appreciate that none of the thousands of visitors to New Zealand over the last twenty or so years would recognise the picture I've painted. The country was transformed in the Eighties by Lange's Labour government and now has a rich and cosmopolitan cultural life. It also has poverty and all the other social problems we associate with inequality.

As for my belief in participatory democracy, I was in a good position to see this principle at work in the field of education. Every New Zealand school was managed by a lay body elected by local parents. These bodies would have only limited influence regarding curriculum and staffing, but this still left much for parents to be involved in. The law required well-publicised elections to these bodies to ensure scope for parental involvement. Reports in the local press of those meetings, for over a period of something like 100 years, show a clear pattern. Say seven committee members were to be elected; typically about five parents would turn up, declare themselves elected, and co-opt two of their mates. There were reports of meeting of over a hundred and of lively debates. Most would refer to some local scandal. Rarely did well-attended meetings indicate a well-run school with which parents wanted to be associated. Parental participation wasn't necessarily a positive or innovative force anyway; dispassionate civil servants or regional bureaucrats were often a greater force for good. My belief in the value of community and participation became more nuanced too.

In brief my research in those early years came to reshape my thinking. I've never recovered my old certainties or found new ones. Naturally these early developments began to shape me as a teacher.

Building on a Shaky Foundation

Once established back in Britain I began to research politics and literature as well as British party politics. One of the earliest ventures was to conduct a survey in the mid-Seventies of the reading habits of Labour MPs, many of whom turned out to be working-class autodidacts. They knew their William Morris, Bernard Shaw and HG Wells as well as their Marx and, of course, their Bible. I went on to interview a dozen or so who had expressed a particular interest in my survey. I asked each if there was any character or situation or event from their reading that they felt had shaped their political philosophy. One became quite animated: "Those bastard pigs from *Animal Farm*...and they're still around, you know, on the backbenches." On whose side, I asked? "Well, both actually, but mostly on ours!" Of the younger MPs who responded to my original questionnaire, a number said they'd little time for reading. Twenty years later that older generation and all it stood for was gone. We are now in the hands of the non-readers.

That older world began to disintegrate in the Seventies with the erosion of the so-called post-war consensus and the shared values that had made it possible; Margaret Thatcher and Keith Joseph read the burial rights. The political landscape that Tony Blair came to shape in his own image set a pattern: 'Cool Britannia', managed on the whole by young men from a privileged background. Blair himself and later Cameron, Osborne, Clegg and Johnson were as far removed from ordinary people and their problems and aspirations as were the Tory leaders attacked by Disraeli in the middle of the nineteenth century. On the other side of the House those working class autodidacts made way for a new breed of young middle class, university educated ex-researchers. And Jeremy Corbyn.

Unless you are amongst the many who apparently have Prime Minister Boris Johnson's personal telephone number, access to leading political figures isn't easy in Britain, at least not in comparison to New Zealand where, at our first meeting my supervisor arranged a meeting for me with the Minister of Education. Thirty years later as a senior academic I returned to New Zealand to pursue research into the effects of electoral reform on the party system .The 'British' first-past-the-post electoral system had been abolished. This involved my interviewing many leading politicians. Whilst in Wellington I met a former colleague from Hull who had joined the priesthood and had been despatched to praise The Lord in New Zealand. When I mentioned that the Prime Minister hadn't responded to my calls for an interview, he promised help. "If you can get down for Mass on Sunday I'll introduce you." I got my interview in the rear pews of the Wellington Basilica. Sometime later I made a second research trip to New Zealand, this time looking at policy formulation during a previous ground-breaking Labour administration, and met a former Prime Minister. Since leaving office David Lange had acquired a reputation as loose cannon. This was the most informative interview I have ever undertaken, grapeshot everywhere, and most of the material too explosive to use - but it taught me a lot about party politics.

Government and Me: Education

I was involved in aspects of secondary education for much of my career. I had a Teaching Diploma; I had taught for a year in a secondary school, I was a Chief Examiner in Politics for an 'A' Level Board for almost 20 years and the Senior Examiner for the International Baccalaureate (IB)'s Extended Essay in Politics for nearly as long. I was able to watch at close quarters, indeed if I may be immodest, play some small part in the development of modularity in the 'A' Level syllabus. Modular 'A' Levels constitute a breaking up of the syllabus into chunks that could be examined at regular intervals through the two-years of an 'A' Level course. Grades would no longer be decided by two examinations set at the end of two years of study. It's said to ease the pressure on students and allow for a wider range of skills to be tested. In my experience there has always been some support for such an approach amongst teachers, though in earlier days probably a minority. But the impetus for reform came from left-wing theorists, advisers within the Department of Education and some of the smaller Examining Boards which might expect to grow their client base by producing syllabuses that seemed more 'user friendly' than the traditional model. As Senior Examiner I was asked by my Board to prepare a modular syllabus. I agreed provided I could work with a committee of half-a-dozen practising teachers.

At our inaugural meeting I asked my colleagues who was in favour of modularity. None was. This was a change driven by theorists. Nevertheless in that lovely Edwardian phrase we put to with a will. We encountered substantial problems: how to enumerate, codify and apportion value to particular skills; how to optimise the timetable for testing them, and finally how to grade and reward those skills, especially since they would be graded at different points over the two years. On a number of occasions we met with civil servants from the Department of Education and their advisers to discuss progress. I raised a serious concern at an early meeting. As well as experienced Secondary teachers, a significant number of 'A' Level markers were recruited from universities or other institutions of Higher and Further Education, whose teaching commitments tended to be complete by the time 'A' Levels were marked, providing a group of highly experienced and skilled markers, few of whom would be in a position to offer their services at other points in the academic year. This would mean recruiting many more examiners inevitably of a lower standard. Had the bureaucrats given any thought to this, I asked? "Your problem!" was the dismissive reply. There have subsequently been continuous disagreements over marking standards. One of the reasons for grade 'inflation' has been the result of poorer and less confidently maintained marking standards.

Another inherent disadvantage is that the standard of work in the early modules will inevitably be lower than that in the later ones. How is this to be factored in? The exam at the end of the two years is supposed to cover all that had been taught, yet it constituted only one module and had to be a shorter paper than its 'A 'Level predecessor and be awarded fewer marks. This examination was supposed to be synoptic *and* cumulative, yet required only two questions to be answered, from a wide choice. Well, enough already: you get the picture: fashionable education theory ignores reality.

Back to the problem of 'A' Levels. It had been always assumed that the reform that most educationalists and most bureaucrats in the Department wanted wasn't modularity at all but some equivalent of the broader based International Baccalaureate (IB). I was invited by friend who knew of my 'A' Level involvement to hear a Junior Minister announce the abolition of 'A' Levels and their replacement by some version of the IB, details to be decided later. In the event the speech made no reference whatever to 'A' Level reform. I was introduced to the Junior Minister over coffee and I told him that I'd travelled all the way down from the land of the bleak north wind just to hear about the abolition of 'A' Levels. Was it true, I asked, that despite strong support in Cabinet, the Iron Lady had let it be known that 'A' Levels would be abolished over her dead body? No comment he replied wistfully. What a golden opportunity for a win-win, some of her cabinet Colleagues must have thought.

Thatcher was, however, willing to support the introduction of what became known as Advanced Supplementary (AS) examinations. These were *not* the same as the AS qualifications which were later awarded at the end of the first year of the new modular 'A' Levels. The originals were free-standing examinations that could be taken alongside traditional 'A's and were based upon a syllabus a little more than half as wide as an 'A' Level syllabus. But crucially they were to be of a comparable standard. Instead of studying for three 'As' students would be encouraged to study for two 'As' and two 'AS'. These new examinations were to be both more imaginative and more focused than the traditional 'As' and to broaden the student's educational experience. This seemed to me a worthwhile compromise and I subsequently recommended to my own Board that we mount an AS in European Union Politics. And we did.

The trouble was the government gave *no* additional funding to schools, so your Politics teacher, for example, would be expected to teach a one-year course in European Union Politics on top of their existing workload without any additional resources. The consequence? Despite the fact that Europe was the flavour of the day, we never had more than 50 or so students across the whole of the UK entering for our new exam, which was withdrawn after three years. The whole idea of AS, a positive attempt to broaden the 'A' Level curriculum, died a completely predictable death. Theory ignores reality...again.

If education is any guide the part played by civil servants and their advisers can be crucial. I had seen the New Zealand Civil Service in action at close quarters. My admittedly brief and more perfunctory contacts with its British counterpart suggest a contrast: the contacts between civil servants and 'user groups' was on a firmer footing in New Zealand. I was having coffee with a junior civil servant in the Education Department in Wellington once when the leader of the NZEI (the union for primary teachers) walked past our table and gave me a smile of acknowledgement. I asked my colleague if he knew him. He told me it was one of his seniors in the Department though he couldn't name him. That's how frequent a visitor this union leader was: he'd become part of the furniture. In Britain close relationships seem largely restricted to old school networks at the higher levels, sometimes of a rather dubious character: the so-called chumocracy. No doubt the British Civil Service exhibits many of the qualities of Confucius' Mandarins but the Whitehall bubble seems even more remote from ordinary life than the Westminster bubble. After all, MPs have their constituents giving them regular earfuls of reality. Maybe it is the size and propinquity of the communities they served that kept the New Zealand civil service I knew out of a bureaucracy bubble. Britain is over-centralised and over-bureaucratised. Almost unique to British culture, to refer to someone as a bureaucrat is to insult them.

Government and Me: Health

Another field of government activity interested me professionally, health. After about eight years at Hull I was approached by a senior colleague in the Department of Social Administration to collaborate with him in preparing an application for research funding for a project in health policy formulation. He had a reputation for delivering successfully on such projects but also was known as something of a martinet and he would be the senior partner. However the project sounded interesting and, after all, I was a big boy now, and so I agreed. At the time I was writing a book on politics and literature and couldn't contribute much for about fifteen months. This didn't please him. Politics and literature seemed a bit dilettantist but he grumpily agreed to wait, suggesting we might arrange meetings in the meantime to sort out a strategy. On the outcome of these meetings Ron put together a successful application for research funding from the ESRC: he knew what he was doing. About a year later, with my manuscript finally submitted to Macmillan, we appointed a research assistant and mapped out our research programme in some detail.

During our meetings over the year I'd noticed that Ron appeared to be getting increasingly less energised, his eyes duller; he began to take more of a back seat in our discussions. and that wasn't Ron's way. His subsequent spiral into serious ill health was dramatic and within six months of the project beginning Ron was no more. We weren't close, so I was losing a valued colleague rather than a friend, but I now found myself as the director of a project that had never been mine in an area of government about which I knew not a lot. Shades of my early PhD days in Wellington! But my research assistant was sharp, hard-working and seemed to know what I wanted him to do before I got round to asking him. As well as a first-class research assistant he became a good friend.

The project that Phil and I undertook involved a study of the evolution of government health policy in the Seventies entailing a detailed analysis of parliamentary debates and the work of relevant parliamentary committees, and a series of interviews with backbench MPs interested in the politics of health. We were concerned not so much to make judgements on the efficacy of government policies as to ascertain the role of ideology and partisanship in the processes of policy formulation. We analysed debates on the Floor of both Houses and in committees. Long story short, we found what we were expecting - don't all researchers? Partisan considerations dominated all aspects of the decision-making processes, except in the Lords. More often than not, we felt obliged to conclude, partisan ideology appeared to be inimical to good government. Our study was published so I suppose we can claim some success.

There were repercussions. A few years after its publication I was approached by a local Health Board to join it as a lay representative. This experience, over five years, contributed substantially to my understanding of how politics operates in the real world. The Chair was a local businessman who saw his main job as being to hold the officers accountable to the Board as representing the community and he succeeded in maintaining a sensible balance between allowing the officers enough elbow room to bustle whilst ensuring general approval for their policies. Of the lay representatives the most involved was the wife of a local farmer who was a key figure in the hierarchy of the local Conservative party.

She and I often sat on a small committee which assessed appeals for release from patients who had been sectioned in the local mental hospital –identified on my Sixties OS map as the County Lunatic Asylum. We would interview the appellants at length with the help of a detailed verbal report from the relevant psychiatrist, and come to a decision regarding release. One young woman in her late twenties seemed to have got her act together and had an encouraging report. I had asked her early on where she proposed to live and was surprised to hear that she would rent a flat in a pleasantly leafy part of town. Was she sure she would be able to afford it on her benefits? My farmer's wife colleague changed the subject. In all other respects she seemed a strong candidate for release but I came back to what seemed to me an unrealistic confidence in her ability to make ends meet. But again my colleague changed the subject. The young woman left and we discussed her case with the psychiatrist. Naturally I returned to the subject of rents but was cut unceremoniously short. "Young man", said my colleague, "what world are you livin' in? She'll be on the game, won't she? She'll have her problems, I don't doubt, but paying rent isn't goin' to be one of 'em. Take your head out of your books, you academics, and you know *nowt*." We allowed the appeal.

Not long after I joined the Board we were faced with what would prove to be our first round of Thatcherite cuts. We were required to shave 5% from our annual budget. Nobody was enthusiastic about the exercise but the chair and his senior officers put on a brave face. We probably could make efficiency savings; the exercise might prove valuable. Maybe it did: we met our target. The government required us to repeat the same exercise the following year. And who was to say it wouldn't be followed by a similar measure the following year? As indeed it was. Lumps of bone, muscle and sinew began to appear in the diminishing amounts of fat we were able to shave off in successive years.

In that first year hospital cleaning was outsourced as were the laundry facilities. I'd spent three months in hospital as an eighteen-year old after a motor cycle accident, and from the time I became conscious of my surroundings I was aware of two women in green outfits whom I took to be junior nurses because they were so solicitous. It was only later that I realised they were cleaners and the little services they performed were acts of kindness. No doubt women provided similar services in our hospitals. Now we were handing them over to a commercial company whose aim would be to make a profit. After the service had been running for about eighteen months I asked for a comparison of the average length in post of a cleaner pre and post outsourcing. Pre-reform it was over two years; post-reform just six weeks. Could they conceivably provide as good a service? It's not especially difficult to save money if you are prepared to sacrifice service.

The laundry outsourcing saga provided another, more graphic example of the perils of theory confronting reality. We were obliged to put our laundry services out to tender, but in-house bidding was encouraged.

Our mental hospital was served by a large Victorian laundry. Built to last forever it could provide 80% of the district's laundry needs; we would have to source the other 20% elsewhere, so ours wasn't the lowest bid. As I remember it, there had been three external bids, two cheaper than the in-house one. Board officers were able to convince their Whitehall superiors that the cheapest was unrealistic and that the middle bid, from a nearby Health Authority should be awarded the contract. The third bid was appreciably higher. The Health Authority got the contract and our Victorian facility was sold off. The arrangement proved unsatisfactory from the outset. We had to deploy staff to go through the laundry when it came back. Much of it had to be sent back and paper alternatives bought to meet the shortfall. It was decided not to renew the contract. Go to the original, cheapest bid, we were told. So we did: the company had gone bust. The response of the highest bidder was that events had shown their original quotation to have been unrealistic and they submitted a new, higher bid. Well, said the officials, you'll just have to use your in-house capacity after all. But it had already been sold! We had to replace it with more expensive and less efficient machinery. Here the quest for efficiency and economy led to exactly the opposite.

Our own quest for savings took us to an interesting place. Most of our surgeons lived in the plusher outskirts west of Hull whereas they mostly worked away, in Driffield or Bridlington for example. And they would travel out and back each day, limiting the number of operations they could undertake. What if, every so often, they were to stay out for the working week? They could perform more operations. Initially the surgeons were reluctant but finally agreed, with the expected increase in productivity. However every additional operation consequent upon greater efficiency put our costs up. We'd looked to efficiency for savings and got the opposite.

Then came target setting. In the NHS waiting times were seen as a crucial measure of efficiency, so targets had to be set; for example, for the length of time between a GP's referral and the patient's appointment, or between diagnosis and outcome. All our waiting times except for orthopaedic surgery were within target and there was only one way to cut waiting times in orthopaedics, to make another specialist appointment. We scrimped and saved even harder and did without here and there and behold: a new orthopaedic surgeon emerged. In no time waiting lists for elective orthopaedic surgery lengthened. *Why*? A number of elderly patients in various stages of need were being treated locally by GPs all-round the district, who knew only too well the limitations of the service. A new surgeon? The dam burst, referrals flooded in and the waiting list rose. Even where theories work they don't always work!

Cumulatively my research led me to the view that governments and those who advise them tend to look out on the world through a prism distorted by ideological theory. I had researched health politics for several years and written a book on the subject. I had my own theories. Experience in the real world however gave me a much keener appreciation of how things really work. My farmer's wife colleague had been right, as usual: take my head out a book, especially one that I'd written myself, and I knew *nowt*. And what was true of me was true of most politicians and their advisors.

Here I Stand... I Think

Surely these experiences must have helped me to shape a coherent political philosophy? Well, sometime in the late '80s, at Hull, I had the privilege of teaching a few miners from the Yorkshire pits who had been made redundant. One took my course in Socialism and Literature. How had he found it? He'd taken the course, he said, to clarify muddled views on major issues, like the proper relationship between the individual and the state. "I finished this course a sight more confused than when I started." I'll drink to that: I would have to say pretty much the same about my career. Some convictions remain, refined over the years. Though I no longer believe in the possibility or even desirability of an equal society, I passionately believe in a profound reduction in existing inequalities. Though I am a supporter of the welfare state I would much prefer a 'welfare society' with greater voluntary involvement encouraged. My faith in Britain's two-party adversarial system of government, however, has failed me entirely.

When I was an undergraduate the textbooks took it for granted that a partisan two-party ideological politics, even one based crudely upon social class, represented the final embodiment of democratic government. It was to be found in all the fullest developed democracies: the UK, the USA, Australia, Canada and New Zealand. (Notice a theme emerging here?) There were a significant number of European states struggling towards 'real' democracy but they were yet to make the crucial advance from the confusions and inefficiencies of the multi-party to the clarity and certainty of a two- party system like ours. We wished them well, especially those plucky Nordics. The two-party system allowed for the forces of progress to compete with those of order and stability within a rule-based parliamentary framework, and to the regular and orderly transfer of power. The natural swing of the pendulum saw first the progressives then the conservatives forming administrations which were inevitably held in some sort of check by Her Majesty's Loyal Opposition. No matter that the contest between progressive and conservative forces, sometimes crudely caricatured as a contest between equality and liberty, had morphed into a contest between those forces which favoured a 'big state' and those which favoured a minimalist state, crudely between organised labour and organised capital. The two-party adversarial system represented mature democracy.

This analysis seemed sound enough to us Politics students in the late Fifties and early Sixties. We only began to question it as post-war British electorates, after six years of 'big state' socialism, began to elect predominantly Conservative governments. There was no natural balance after all. In 1960 Mark Abrams wrote a little bombshell of a book entitled *Must Labour Lose?* in which the influence of organised labour was shown to be diminishing and likely to continue to diminish, making electoral victory for a traditional Labour party increasingly difficult. Moreover, some of these formerly patronised European democracies seemed to be faring well despite their pram full of parties and resultant coalition governments. They showed no signs of even wanting to develop into

163

mature two-party systems like the Anglo-Saxons. What's more, they were beginning to prosper economically to a greater extent than Britain. I was of the generation which finally recognised that in the two-party adversarial model we had been sold a pup.

Every sliver of relevant research, every slice of active involvement that I've undertaken has reinforced my belief that our present system of government is incapable of meeting the unparalleled challenges facing Britain, and indeed the world. I am convinced that adversarial two-party politics have become inimical to good government. I'm not suggesting that parties be banned. It's naked adversarialism I want to be rid of and electoral reform might do the job. I have come to believe that the policy-making process has to be restructured so as to embody a much more representative *balance* with inputs from the government of the day, local government, the general public, the civil service and relevant interest groups. The key to any effective balance of these forces is that it must be on-going and it must be transparent. Policy making should *evolve* through the transparent interaction of the forces in that balance put in place and maintained by a democratically elected national government. Alexander Pope penned a famous couplet about only fools contesting *forms* of government. "What e'er is best administered is best", he concluded. Neat but wrong. So much actually hangs upon forms of government. It wouldn't be appropriate to go into detail here, but the balanced 'form' I'm in favour of would, for example, devolve more power to regions under the mayoral system, would restructure, repurpose and *rename* the House of Lords. And the government of the day would be likely to comprise a coalition in which party ideology could not dominate.

No such balanced form of government would have thought it sensible to privatise water or the railways. Or to sell off nearly two million council houses without replacing them. Or mess about with the structure and funding of the health service or the education system every few years as result of some ill-considered ideological theory. Or crucially to hand a massively important and complex issue like Brexit to be decided by those least able to make a balanced judgement, the general public (and I mean *all of us*, not just Brexiteers). Public opinion is a much more complex phenomenon than your average punter might think. When nineteenth-century writers recommended a decisive role for public opinion in decision making they had something more subtle and complex in mind than referendums. Rousseau had already muddied the waters comprehensively by redefining public opinion as the 'general will'. Read Henrik Ibsen on popular majorities in *Enemy of the People*, or asks Brutus about the wisdom of crowds. It was the crowd that condemned Jesus Christ to crucifixion and chose to release the criminal Barabbas. The notion of governing through balance represents a far truer reflection of what could realistically be called 'public opinion' than any snapshot poll or one-off referendum. There are far more sophisticated methods for measuring 'real' public opinion than these.

The present system whereby two dysfunctional political parties wage endless battles trading futile promises aimed at short-term political advantage and involving an over centralised state is anathema to good, balanced government in the interests of all the people, a travesty of the principle of truly representative government. Besides, two-party partisan adversarial politics no longer has any purchase or relevance since so few of the major issues of today are amenable to partisan politics. You can't have two sets of competing and interchanging policies on climate change, energy policy, health or education – or indeed anything that matters. Far from being a model for others to copy, our adversarial system has become an insurmountable obstacle to good government today.

I've come to the conclusion that my Korean student in Hull all those years ago wasn't so far wrong when he pointed out the hollowness of Britain's claim to be a vibrant and inclusive democracy when all we can hope for is an 'erection' every five years. The political scientist Andrew Gamble wrote that the two-party system only really worked when it wasn't working, for example during the years of the post-war consensus when there didn't appear to be much difference between the policies of the major parties. My research experience endorses that judgement and makes me want to add that I continually found evidence that the insidious influence of theories attached to political ideologies, what George Orwell called 'smelly little orthodoxies' led to bad government. I want to conclude with a story that illustrates the fact that reality and theory inhabit different universes indicating the likely consequences of this for good government.

What follows is an account of an exchange, as I remember it, from an early radio phone-in programme featuring a former Minister of Health, Enoch Powell and a member of the public. Phoning from Lancashire a woman asked Powell if he believed in legislating to secure equal pay for women. Mr Powell believed in equal pay for equal work but argued that unequal pay was unsustainable in any truly competitive economy, so it would be unnecessary to involve the law. But, the caller, a millworker, continued, she was getting paid only two thirds as much as a male acquaintance doing the same job.

"My dear lady," Powell patiently explained in those memorably crafted sentences delivered in his incongruous, artisanal Midlands accent, "allow me to explain how that simply cannot be. If your employer discovered that a woman could do the same work as a man for two thirds the pay, and with no diminution of quality, he would go out of his way to employ as many women as he could. As a consequence he would sooner or later gain a substantial competitive advantage over his rivals and in turn other mill owners would be obliged to copy his practice and maximise the number of women on their pay rolls. Before long, every mill in the country would be staffed largely by women. Manifestly this is not happening. So unequal pay for equal work is simply unsustainable and indeed unfeasible. I'm afraid, dear lady, you must be mistaken." Then came an eruption from Lancashire: "But Mr Powell, I've seen his bloody pay slip!"

I Rest My Case

My research shaped the person and the teacher that I became. I hope it made me a more rounded person; I'm certain it made me a better teacher. Here is a comment from an anonymised appraisal from the last tutorial class of the last semester of my teaching career. In those few lines that student more or less justified my entire career as a teacher, so I hope it was the fruit of mature reflection. "These classes were brilliant. By the end of the unit, I thought I understood more about how politics works, more about what matters. This is what I'd thought all university courses were going to be like." But I'm an academic, always looking for the balanced picture. A couple of years earlier, a student appraising my first-year lectures had asked: "What gives Professor Spring the idea that stitching a series of anecdotes together constitutes a lecture?" Well let me nail my standard to the masthead, I'd go for anecdotes over power points every time.

Postscript

As I complete this book and look back on my academic career, I feel some level of reassurance that for all their shortcomings the Concrete Towers have never given up on the mission that I spoke of at the beginning - sustaining (and redefining!) our cultural heritage and making it available to a far wider range of students, and marrying that heritage to a broad range of socially relevant intellectual skills - but year by year the pressures only grow. Recently, the role and functions of the Concrete Towers have been put in the spotlight by the pandemic, which ravaged higher education as much as any other sector in 2020. When the worst is behind us, things will not simply go back to 'normal'. The impact of technologies on higher education has been felt over the last decade at least, but never more acutely than during the pandemic. We need seriously to consider the uses *and limits* of technology when ascertaining the proper role and function of the Concrete Towers in our modern world, and we need to do it by involving the forces that make up the balance I've been writing about and not by applying smelly little orthodoxies cultivated within Whitehall, the party machines or various think tanks. Moreover we need to establish the proper purpose of education in a Concrete Tower. We especially need to confront as an educational community those corrosive issues around freedom of speech and cultural legacy that have emerged in recent years. How appropriate that this should all be happening at a time when the very future of concrete is under scrutiny because of the environmental damage its manufacture causes.